DATE DUE

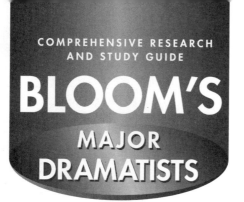

COMPREHENSIVE RESEARCH
AND STUDY GUIDE

BLOOM'S
MAJOR
DRAMATISTS

Eugene
O'Neill

EDITED AND WITH AN
INTRODUCTION BY HAROLD BLOOM

CURRENTLY AVAILABLE

BLOOM'S MAJOR DRAMATISTS

Anton Chekhov
Henrik Ibsen
Arthur Miller
Eugene O'Neill
Shakespeare's Comedies
Shakespeare's Histories
Shakespeare's Romances
Shakespeare's Tragedies
George Bernard Shaw
Tennessee Williams

BLOOM'S MAJOR NOVELISTS

Jane Austen
The Brontës
Willa Cather
Charles Dickens
William Faulkner
F. Scott Fitzgerald
Nathaniel Hawthorne
Ernest Hemingway
Toni Morrison
John Steinbeck
Mark Twain
Alice Walker

BLOOM'S MAJOR SHORT STORY WRITERS

William Faulkner
F. Scott Fitzgerald
Ernest Hemingway
O. Henry
James Joyce
Herman Melville
Flannery O'Connor
Edgar Allan Poe
J. D. Salinger
John Steinbeck
Mark Twain
Eudora Welty

BLOOM'S MAJOR WORLD POETS

Geoffrey Chaucer
Emily Dickinson
John Donne
T. S. Eliot
Robert Frost
Langston Hughes
John Milton
Edgar Allan Poe
Shakespeare's Poems & Sonnets
Alfred, Lord Tennyson
Walt Whitman
William Wordsworth

BLOOM'S NOTES

The Adventures of Huckleberry Finn
Aeneid
The Age of Innocence
Animal Farm
The Autobiography of Malcolm X
The Awakening
Beloved
Beowulf
Billy Budd, Benito Cereno, & Bartleby the Scrivener
Brave New World
The Catcher in the Rye
Crime and Punishment
The Crucible

Death of a Salesman
A Farewell to Arms
Frankenstein
The Grapes of Wrath
Great Expectations
The Great Gatsby
Gulliver's Travels
Hamlet
Heart of Darkness & The Secret Sharer
Henry IV, Part One
I Know Why the Caged Bird Sings
Iliad
Inferno
Invisible Man
Jane Eyre
Julius Caesar

King Lear
Lord of the Flies
Macbeth
A Midsummer Night's Dream
Moby-Dick
Native Son
Nineteen Eighty-Four
Odyssey
Oedipus Plays
Of Mice and Men
The Old Man and the Sea
Othello
Paradise Lost
A Portrait of the Artist as a Young Man
The Portrait of a Lady

Pride and Prejudice
The Red Badge of Courage
Romeo and Juliet
The Scarlet Letter
Silas Marner
The Sound and the Fury
The Sun Also Rises
A Tale of Two Cities
Tess of the D'Urbervilles
Their Eyes Were Watching God
To Kill a Mockingbird
Uncle Tom's Cabin
Wuthering Heights

COMPREHENSIVE RESEARCH
AND STUDY GUIDE

BLOOM'S

MAJOR
DRAMATISTS

*Eugene
O'Neill*

EDITED AND WITH AN INTRODUCTION
BY HAROLD BLOOM

© 2000 by Chelsea House Publishers, a division of Main Line Book Co.

Introduction © 2000 by Harold Bloom

Printed and bound in the United States of America.

First Printing
1 3 5 7 9 8 6 4 2

Library of Congress Cataloging-in-Publication Data
applied for
ISBN 0-7910-5245-1

Chelsea House Publishers
1974 Sproul Road, Suite 400
Broomall, PA 19008-0914

The Chelsea House world wide web
address is www.chelseahouse.com

Contributing Editor: Erica DaCosta

Contents

User's Guide

This volume is designed to present biographical, critical, and bibliographical information on the author's best-known or most important works. Following Harold Bloom's editor's note and introduction is a detailed biography of the author, discussing major life events and important literary accomplishments. A plot summary of each play follows, tracing significant themes, patterns, and motifs in the work.

A selection of critical extracts, derived from previously published material from leading critics, analyzes aspects of each play. The extracts consist of statements from the author, if available, early reviews of the work, and later evaluations up to the present. A bibliography of the author's writings (including a complete list of all works written, cowritten, edited, and translated), a list of additional books and articles on the author and his or her work, and an index of themes and ideas in the author's writings conclude the volume.

~

Harold Bloom is Sterling Professor of the Humanities at Yale University and Henry W. and Albert A. Berg Professor of English at the New York University Graduate School. He is the author of over 20 books and the editor of more than 30 anthologies of literary criticism.

Professor Bloom's works include *Shelley's Mythmaking* (1959), *The Visionary Company* (1961), *Blake's Apocalypse* (1963), *Yeats* (1970), *A Map of Misreading* (1975), *Kabbalah and Criticism* (1975), and *Agon: Toward a Theory of Revisionism* (1982). *The Anxiety of Influence* (1973) sets forth Professor Bloom's provocative theory of the literary relationships between the great writers and their predecessors. His most recent books include *The American Religion* (1992), *The Western Canon* (1994), *Omens of Millennium: The Gnosis of Angels, Dreams, and Resurrection* (1996), and *Shakespeare: The Invention of the Human* (1998), a finalist for the 1998 National Book Award.

Professor Bloom earned his Ph.D. from Yale University in 1955 and has served on the Yale faculty since then. He is a 1985 MacArthur Foundation Award recipient, served as the Charles Eliot Norton Professor of Poetry at Harvard University in 1987–88, and has received honorary degrees from the universities of Rome and Bologna. In 1999, Professor Bloom received the prestigious American Academy of Arts and Letters Gold Medal for Criticism.

Currently, Harold Bloom is the editor of numerous Chelsea House volumes of literary criticism, including the series BLOOM'S NOTES, BLOOM'S MAJOR SHORT STORY WRITERS, BLOOM'S MAJOR POETS, MAJOR LITERARY CHARACTERS, MODERN CRITICAL VIEWS, MODERN CRITICAL INTERPRETATIONS, and WOMEN WRITERS OF ENGLISH AND THEIR WORKS.

Editor's Note

My Introduction centers upon the Strindbergian *The Iceman Cometh,* and on its superiority as theater to the experience of reading it.

The early *Anna Christie* is illuminated by Neill's biographers, the Gelbs, and by Travis Bogard's meditation upon the heroine.

Eric Bentley, our most distinguished dramatic critic, does his best to admire *The Iceman Cometh,* a play usefully commented upon here in all the Critical Views, Doris Falk's in particular.

Long Day's Journey Into Night is reviewed by Kenneth Tynan and by Harold Churman. Richard B. Sewall's defense of the play as tragedy has assumed classic status.

Introduction

HAROLD BLOOM

Eugene O'Neill's judgment upon his country was: "We are tragedy." Nearly a half-century after the playwright's death, I would be inclined to revise that into: "We are farce." O'Neill's despair of American illusions was constant and impressive, but can it be called a vision of America, in the antithetical senses in which Tennessee Williams and Arthur Miller dramatically achieve visions of our nation? In the literary sense, O'Neill had little to do with American tradition. Partly this is because we had no important playwright before O'Neill. His resort to Henrik Ibsen, and even more to Ibsen's rival, August Strindberg, was crucial for his art. *The Iceman Cometh* owes much to Strindberg's *The Dance of Death,* and something to Ibsen insofar as Hickey authentically is a deidealizer. Schopenhauer, Nietzsche, and Freud hover in the intellectual background of *Iceman,* Schopenhauer in particular. Of American intellectual or literary tradition, O'Neill was either hostile or ignorant. Without much knowing Emerson, O'Neill can be said to destroy, where he can, the American credo of Self-Reliance.

An unbelieving Irish Catholic, who yet retained the puritanism of his religious heritage, O'Neill judged that the United States had failed to achieve spiritual reality. The judgment is peculiar, partly because O'Neill knew nothing about the American Religion, which is Evangelical, personal, and both Gnostic and Orphic. Hickey, O'Neill's nihilistic protagonist, comes to destroy hope because he judges it to be more pernicious than despair. What makes Hickey dramatically interesting is his clashing realizations that the derelicts need to be divested of their hope, but also that they need their "pipe dreams" or illusions if they are to survive. O'Neill's "pipe dream" was to believe that any nation could achieve spiritual "reality" as such.

Did Hickey murder his wife because of love, or hatred? Is he too motivated by hope, or by despair? We never know, and this is all to the good, since our ignorance augments drama. Larry Slade, in contrast, is one of Neill's major failures in characterization. His condemnation of the mother-betraying Parritt to a suicide's death is persuasive neither as action nor as reflection. O'Neill's own spiritual incoherence emerges clearly in his surrogate, Slade, who thinks himself a convert to Hickey's Will-to-Die, yet remains a lapsed Catholic, yearning for grace. We are left with stirring theater, but with a spiritual enigma. ❀

Biography of
Eugene O'Neill

Eugene Gladstone O'Neill was born in New York City on October 16, 1888. His father, James O'Neill, was a popular romantic actor, who exposed his son to the theater at a very early age. O'Neill entered Princeton in 1906, after attending a Catholic boarding school and a preparatory school in Connecticut, but within a year he had flunked out and had taken up an adventurous life, working variously as a seaman, gold prospector, journalist, and actor.

O'Neill wrote his first play, *The Web*, in the winter of 1913–14. By 1916 he had become associated with the Provincetown Players, who in the following three years produced many of his plays, including *Bound East for Cardiff* (1916) and *The Moon of the Caribbees* (1918). His first great success came in 1920 with the Broadway production of *Beyond the Horizon*, which won O'Neill a Pulitzer Prize. He followed this with several other naturalistic tragedies with American settings; these were not tragedies of destiny or fate, but of personal psychology. They include *Chris Christopherson* (1920), rewritten as *Anna Christie* (1921; Pulitzer Prize); *Diff'rent* (1920); *Gold* (1921); *The Straw* (1921); and *The First Man* (1922). O'Neill also created two experiments in symbolic expressionism: *The Emperor Jones* (1920) and *The Hairy Ape* (1922). After *The Hairy Ape* he returned to a naturalistic approach with *All God's Chillun Got Wings* (1924) and *Desire under the Elms* (1924).

The political, *Fountain* (1925) was followed by *The Great God Brown* (1926), in which masks are worn; *Lazarus Laughed* (1927), featuring choral chanting; *Marco Millions* (1928); *Strange Interlude* (1928, Pulitzer Prize), in which O'Neill experimented with a stream-of-consciousness technique; and *Dynamo* (1929). *Mourning Becomes Electra*, an adaptation of Aeschylus' theme, followed in 1931. *Ah, Wilderness!* (1933), a light comedy, and *Days Without End* (1934) were the last plays to be produced for many years, although O'Neill worked on several others, including *The Iceman Cometh* (1946). In 1936 he was awarded the Nobel Prize for Literature.

O'Neill's masterpiece *Long Day's Journey Into Night*, a semi-autobiographical family tragedy, was written in 1940–41, and produced posthumously in 1956. *A Moon for the Misbegotten,* his last play, was written by 1943 and produced in 1947. After O'Neill's death in 1953 a number of other plays were posthumously produced; *Hughie,* a one-act character study, was acted in 1958, and two plays from a projected eleven-play cycle, *A Tale of Possessors Self-Dispossed,* were also produced: *A Touch of the Poet* (published 1957, acted 1958) and its sequel *More Stately Mansions* (1964). His *Poems* were collected in 1979.

In creating a drama that attempted to confront social and moral issues realistically and with force, O'Neill, despite his debt to Strindberg and Ibsen and his somewhat simplistic use of the ideas of Freud, Jung, and others, made an original contribution to the American stage, and has generally been considered his country's greatest playwright. ❀

Plot Summary of
Anna Christie

Eugene O'Neill came to regard *Anna Christie* as his worst play, though he resisted the charge that it was pat and sentimental. When the play was first produced, critics accused O'Neill of pandering to popular tastes, pointing specifically to the ending, which was not only unusually optimistic for O'Neill but also inconsistent with the tone of the rest of the play. O'Neill, on the other hand, insisted that the seemingly happy ending was underscored by the dark prospects that lay ahead for the newlyweds: "In the last few minutes of '*Anna Christie*' I tried to show the dramatic gathering of new forces out of the old," O'Neill told the *New York Times* in December 1921. "I wanted to have the audience leave with a deep feeling of life flowing on, of the past which is never the past—but always the birth of the future—of a problem solved for the moment but by the very nature of its solution involving new problems."

Anna Christie was the last version of a play originally titled and produced as *Chris Christopherson*. Throughout the playwright's extensive revisions, the focus of the drama shifted from Chris Christopherson, the father, to Anna, his daughter. O'Neill based the character of Chris on an old sailor he had once known whose suspicion of, and contempt for, the sea had grown steadily until he attempted to leave the life altogether. Life on land proved so foreign to him, however, that he was forced to accept a job as a captain of a barge—a humiliating defeat for a career sailor. When the barge was docked, the man spent much of his time in "Jimmy-the-Priest's" saloon, drinking cheap whiskey and denouncing the sea. His sad story ended one Christmas when, in a drunken stupor, he fell to the ice and froze to death.

In *Anna Christie*, Chris Christopherson has unhappily surrendered his life to the sea. He blames the sea for ruining the lives of all those who belong to it, though he inadvertently expresses a love for its awesome beauty and mystery. For most of O'Neill's sailor characters, the sea is a force of God and the source of their own welfare, but it also ties them to itself by requiring submission to its power.

Act I opens in Johnny-the-Priest's saloon, where the bar owner and his employee, Larry, muse over a letter that has just been delivered for Christopher Christopherson, whom they call "Chris."

Shortly after it arrives, Chris himself enters the bar with a woman, Marthy Owen, with whom he is involved. The letter is from his daughter, Anna, whom he has not seen in 15 years. Anna writes that she got sick on her job in St. Paul, Minnesota, and is coming to see him. When Larry asks why he hasn't seen her in so long, Chris explains that since he is "sailor fallar," he was often away on voyages, and when his wife, Anna's mother, died, he sent her to live with relatives in Minnesota. His reason for staying out of his daughter's day-to-day life is related to his feelings about life at sea, which he repeats throughout the play: "Ay tank it's better Anna live on farm," Chris says, "den she don't know dat old davil, sea, she don't know fader like me."

After a brief scene in which Chris agonizes over how to tell Marthy that she cannot live with him while his daughter is visiting, we learn the truth about Anna. Chris has gone off at Marthy's urging to get something to eat before his daughter's arrival, and a young woman, who is apparently a prostitute, comes into the bar. She strikes up a conversation with Marthy who, before long, guesses the woman's identity—and her profession. Anna has come here in the hope that her father can provide room and board while she recuperates from an illness she developed while in prison for prostitution.

Anna has grown up lonely and abused. Her relatives worked her hard, and when she was 16 one of her cousins raped her. Although she fled to the city and did work as a nurse's assistant for a time, she eventually drifted into prostitution. Not only has Anna kept the truth from her father, but he has also lied to her, telling her in letters that he was a janitor rather than the captain of a coal barge called the *Simeon Winthrop*. Marthy admits to knowing Chris and tells Anna that he is "as good an old guy as ever walked on two feet."

When Chris enters the bar, Marthy makes a quick exit, warning Chris to "Treat her right, see? She's been sick." After a few awkward moments, father and daughter warm to one another. When Anna asks Chris why he never visited her when she was growing up, he tries to explain that although he longed to return to his family in Sweden at the end of each voyage, something always prevented it. He continually signed up for new voyages to South America, Australia, China, and many other ports of call, but he never signed on a ship bound for Sweden. He cannot explain it, he says, except to claim that it is the fault of the sea, as was the death of his wife and the drownings of both of his sons, Anna's brothers, who were also sailors: "Dat ole davil sea make [sailors] crazy fools with her dirty tricks. It's so," Chris claims. After the loss of most of his family, Chris says, he thought it best to keep Anna distant from him and all things related to the sea.

But Anna does not think his explanation is valid. "Then you think the sea's to blame for everything?" she exclaims. "Well, you're still working on it, ain't you?" Chris claims the barge job is not a genuine sea job and Anna finds this logic even more bewildering, but she accepts it because of her fondness for Chris and her desire to remain near him. Chris too is eager to keep his daughter with him, telling her that he has no one else in the world but her. In an effort to convince her to go with him on the barge, he describes the sea in a very different light. "You don't know how nice it's on barge, Anna. Tug come and ve gat towed out on voyage—yust water all round, and sun, and fresh air, and good grub for make you strong, healthy gel. You see many tangs you don't see before. You gat moonlight at night, maybe; see steamer pass; see schooner make sail—see everytang dat's pooty." Thinking that she could use such a vacation, Anna agrees to give it a try. But when her father begins treating her as though she were still a young, innocent girl—he first offers to get her a drink of ginger ale or sarsaparilla before agreeing that a glass of port would help her appetite—she nearly leaves him behind and rushes out of the bar.

Act II opens in Provincetown on the *Simeon Winthrop* 10 days after father and daughter meet. Anna, who has decided to travel with her father on the barge, has become captivated by the sea and feels cleansed by it. Her troubled past seems wiped away, and she tells her father she would work on the sea if she were a man. "I don't wonder you always been a sailor," she says to him. But Chris is disturbed by her new enthusiasm for the sea. "Ay tank Ay'm damn fool for bring you on voyage," he tells his daughter. She asks whether the men in their family were all sailors, and whether the women all married sailors, and Chris says that both are true. His father died aboard a ship, and of his three brothers, all of whom were sailors, two were lost at sea; his mother died while her sons were on voyages. Chris has begun to regret taking Anna along, because he sees that she has now become "infected" with a love of the sea. "Why d'you s'pose I feel so—so—like I'd found something I'd missed and been looking for—'s if this was the right place for me to fit in?" she asks her father. "And I feel clean, somehow. . . . And I feel happy for once . . . happier than I ever been anywhere before!"

The sea proves itself mischievous at the very least when Chris is suddenly hailed by the survivors of a wrecked steamer, who have been adrift for days. Among them is an Irish stoker named Mat Burke, who at first mistakes Anna for a waterfront prostitute, but soon becomes smitten with her after he learns that she is accompanying her father on the barge. Before long, he proposes marriage. "I'm telling you there's the will of God in it," he says, "that brought me safe through the storm and fog to the wan spot in the world where you was!" Mat's attitude toward his profession is very different from Chris's—he views himself as a powerful force that is strong enough to overcome what the sea can do to him. "It's only on the sea you'd find rale men with guts is fit to wed with fine, high-tempered girls the like of yourself," he tells Anna. Chris comes out of the cabin and, seeing a strange sailor so close to his daughter, orders the man to bed. As Act II ends he shakes his fist at the "damn ole davil," the sea, for bringing Mat and Anna together, and vows that he will not let them marry.

Act III opens in the interior of the barge a week later, as the *Simeon Winthrop* is docked in Boston. Anna and Chris are tense and anxious, and we soon learn that the cause of their disharmony is Anna's relationship with Mat Burke. She has become harshly critical of her father; he in turn complains that she spends all her time with Burke, who is a terrible influence on her. "Dem fallars dat vork below shoveling coal vas de dirtiest, rough gang of no-good fallars in vorld!" he cries. Hesitatingly, Chris asks Anna whether she loves Mat and is going to marry him, and Anna replies that she might have some years ago, but now she "ain't got the heart to fool him." She leaves to take a walk, asking her father to tell Mat where she is.

Mat comes in and tells Chris that he intends to marry Anna that very day. They begin to argue, and Mat briefly placates Chris by asking him why he is against the marriage. Chris tells him that she is all he has, that he doesn't want to be left alone again, but Mat will not agree to leave her alone. The discussion quickly escalates into an argument, with Mat accusing Chris of cowardice: "You've swallowed the anchor," he tells him. "The sea give you a clout once knocked you down, and you're not man enough to get up for another." Chris attacks Mat with a knife, but Mat disarms him just as Anna returns to the cabin.

Anna demands to know the reason for their argument, and when she learns that Mat has told her father that he plans to marry her, she is overwhelmed by the force of Mat's devotion. She is terrified to confess that she was once a prostitute, but she also realizes that she cannot marry Mat and keep her former life a secret. To Chris's delight, she tells Mat that she cannot marry him. Chris and Mat begin arguing again as though she were property, and finally Anna has had enough. She tells them both about her past.

Chris is stunned. He finally realizes that the "safety" of growing up on land was an illusion for Anna. And suddenly, he believes it is best for her to marry Mat. Mat himself is devastated, and despite his promises to stick by her no matter what she had to tell him, he cannot bear the thought of her former life. "Will you believe it if I tell you that loving you has made me clean?" Anna begs, but Mat curses her and runs off to get drunk. Chris, horrified at a situation that he believes he could have prevented, does not condemn Anna; instead, he once again blames the sea, which brought Mat to them and resulted in Anna's confession. He does not want Anna to leave, however; and asks whether she'll wait before he goes off to the saloons as well.

Act IV opens once again in the cabin, two days later, as Anna sits, despondent, dressed in her traveling clothes. Chris enters, having come back for the first time since his daughter's disclosure. He learns that she went ashore to try to catch a train to New York, but then decided not to go until the following day. Chris pleads with her to stay, telling her that he now realizes it was his fault that bad things happened to her, and he also realizes that if Mat truly makes her happy she should marry him. Anna forgives him, but as she points out, it's too late for her to marry Mat. Chris tells her that he has "solved" their problem by getting his old job back as bo'sun on a ship called the *Londonderry*. He will no longer make her life "sorry" the way he did her mother's. Anna points out that he is once again escaping his responsibility as a father by leaving her, but Chris explains that his pay will be sent to her while he's away.

After Chris goes to bed, Mat bursts into the cabin. He had sworn to sign up on a ship that would take him as far away from her as possible, and when she questions him about it she discovers that he has signed on to the *Londonderry,* the steamer on which Chris will be an officer. Mat begs to know that she has never loved another man and gives her a small wooden crucifix of his mother's on which to swear. Anna is sincere when she gives him his promise, and Burke is eager to forgive past transgressions. As they finally agree to marry the following morning, Chris comes from the bedroom with a beer, calling for a congratulatory drink. Mat then learns that he is sailing on the same ship as his future father-in-law. At first he accuses Chris of deserting his daughter again, but Anna declares that she wants him to go and that it's where he belongs, and also that Mat must go to earn money for them. "I'll get used to it," she says of living alone. "I'll get a little house somewhere and I'll make a regular place for you two to come back to,—wait and see." Chris and Burke are reconciled but Chris retains his sense of foreboding. In the end they drink: "Here's to the sea, no matter what!"

Chris, a childish and irresponsible man, full of self-indulgent superstition and convenient excuses, nevertheless loves his daughter and truly regrets the pain he has caused. Mat's acceptance of Anna's past seems contrived; his blind love for Anna remains idealistic and thus presents the prospect of marital difficulties. At best, the future of this new "family" is unclear. O'Neill suggests this uncertainty in the last words of the play, as Chris remarks somberly, "Fog, fog, fog, all bloody time. You can't see where you vas going, no. Only dat ole davil, sea—she knows!" ❁

List of Characters in
Anna Christie

Christopher Christopherson, a Swede, has been a sailor since he was a child and was once an officer, but at 50, he is now captain of the coal barge the *Simeon Winthrop*. He has an almost religious awe of the sea, referring to it frequently as "that ole davil sea." For Chris, the sea is a malevolent force that has ruined the lives of generations of his family members, and in an effort to protect his daughter from this force he sends her to live with relatives on a farm in the Midwest.

Anna Christopherson, Chris's only daughter, is the sole remaining member of his family, his sons and wife having died years earlier. As the play opens, Anna, who calls herself Anna Christie, is reentering her father's life after 15 years. Abused by her relatives and left on her own, Anna turned to prostitution; she is visiting her father to seek his help in recovering from an unspecified illness.

Mat Burke, an Irish stoker, is one of four survivors of a steamer accident who are rescued by Chris and given shelter on his barge. He loves the sea and feels a power over it in a way that Chris does not or will not admit, and this trait is partly what draws Anna to him.

"Johnny-the-Priest" is the owner and bartender of a saloon near South Street, New York City. He is based on a person of the same occupation and nickname whom O'Neill knew in his youth.

Marthy Owen, a waterfront prostitute, lives on the *Simeon Winthrop* with Chris but leaves when Anna arrives.

Larry is a bartender at Johnny-the-Priest's saloon.

Two Longshoremen are incidental characters who appear at the opening of the play in Johnny-the-Priest's saloon.

A **Postman** delivers the letter from Anna to her father at the opening of the play.

Johnson is a deckhand on Chris's barge.

Three Men of a Steamer's Crew are, like Mat Burke, survivors of a shipwreck who take refuge on Chris's barge. ❀

Critical Views on
Anna Christie

EDWIN ENGEL ON FATE AND THE CHRISTOPHERSON
FAMILY

[Edwin Engel is a theater critic and lecturer at Harvard University. In this excerpt, Engel discusses the Christopherson
family as victims of a sinister fate.]

The house of Christopherson is simply the inexplicable victim of
fate—not a fickle fate, nor a blind one, but a sinister one.

> All men in our village on coast, Sveden, go to sea. Ain't
> nutting else for dem to do. My fa'der die on board ship in
> Indian Ocean. He's buried at sea. Ay don't never know
> him only little bit. Den my tree bro'der, older'n me, dey
> go on ships. Den Ay go, too. Den my mo'der she's left all
> 'lone. Ve vas all avay on voyage when she die. (*He pauses
> sadly*) Two my bro'der dey gat lost on fishing boat same
> like your bro'ders vas drowned. My oder bro'der, he save
> money, give up sea, den he die home in bed. He's only
> one dat ole davil don't kill. (*Defiantly*) But me, Ay bet you
> Ay die ashore in bed, too!

The action of the play concerns the discovery of an additional
victim of the "davil sea," Chris' daughter Anna, who, although she
was kept far inland, in Minnesota, was affected nevertheless by the
relentless evil force. And with the arrival of Anna from the Middle
West a new episode in the Christopherson struggle begins, with the
sea inexorably drawing its prey to their doom. Chris had thought
that his daughter was safe on a farm, but the sailor's conception of
rural life, wistfully expressed in the Glencairn plays, is once again
revealed to be completely erroneous. "Your bunk about the farm
being so fine!" Anna violently says to her father. "Didn't I write you
year after year how rotten it was and what a dirty slave them cousins
made of me?" Had Anna not been pursued by the Christopherson
fate she might have avoided the degradation that came to her on her
farm refuge where one of her cousins "started me wrong. (*Loudly*) It
wasn't none of my fault. I hated him worse'n hell and he knew it. But
he was big and strong—"

That was why I run away from the farm. That was what
made me get a yob as nurse girl in St. Paul. (*With a hard,
mocking laugh*) And you think that was a nice yob for a
girl, too, don't you? (*Sarcastically*) With all them nice
inland fellers yust looking for a chance to marry me, I
s'pose. Marry me? What a chance! They wasn't looking
for marrying . . . I'm owning up to everything fair and
square. I was caged in, I tell you—yust like in yail—listening to 'em bawling and crying day and night—when I
wanted to be out—and I was lonesome—lonesome as
hell! (*With a sudden weariness in her voice*) So I gave up
finally. What was the use? ⟨ . . .⟩

When, early in the first act, Chris, Oedipus-like, angrily
responds to the bartender's prophecy that Anna is destined to
marry a sailor, the imminent conflict with fate becomes clearly
defined. In the second act the spectator is prepared for the event
when Anna exults in her sea environment, sensing somewhat mys-
tically that she has been there before. Chris' grim foreboding that
something is about to happen is confirmed, as is the prediction of
the bartender, when the "davil sea" sends the shipwrecked sailor,
Mat Burke, upon the scene. Burke, exhausted as he is, proceeds
almost at once to make love to Anna, even proposing marriage.
The act ends as Chris *turns suddenly and shakes his fist out at the
sea*—[and] *with bitter hatred* says, "Dat's your dirty trick, damn
old davil, you! (*then in a frenzy of rage*) But, py God, you don't do
dat! Not while Ay'm living! No, py God, you don't!"

In the third act occurs the struggle between the father and the
sea-borne lover for possession of Anna. Burke's ardent love-
making and passion for the sea overwhelm her. She *laughs helplessly,* and, *with a sudden joyous defiance,* confesses her love for
him, assuring him that she has never loved a man in her life
before, that he "can always believe that—no matter what happens." What does happen is that she refuses to marry him until
she tells him about her sordid past. Although he had insisted that
she is "the wan woman in the world for me, and I can't live
without her now" and although he had dreamed of their having "a
grand, beautiful life together" to the end of their days, he is overcome with revulsion upon her revelation and rushes off to drink
"sloos of whiskey." It is obvious that by this time the distress of a

whore, in love with an incredible Irish sailor, has displaced the somber theme of a family's struggle with fate.

—Edwin Engel, *The Haunted Heroes of Eugene O'Neill* (Cambridge, MA: Harvard University Press, 1953): pp. 284–286

ARTHUR AND BARBARA GELB ON O'NEILL'S TREATMENT OF PROSTITUTES

[Arthur Gelb is president of the *New York Times* Company Foundation and a former managing editor of the *New York Times*. In this excerpt, the Gelbs discuss O'Neill's depiction of prostitutes in *Anna Christie* and many of his other plays.]

O'Neill made a firsthand study of young girls with painted faces and sad histories.

"Those babes gave me some of the best laughs I've ever had," he once confided to George Jean Nathan, "and to the future profit of many a dramatic scene."

The heroine of *Anna Christie* is a prostitute, and a total of fourteen streetwalkers ply their trade in seven other of his published plays; additional prostitutes figure as offstage characters in another five plays.

Although O'Neill acknowledged their function, he continued to be far more interested in their souls. Having rejected Jamie's view that they were fascinating vampires, he conceived of them as children of fate. For the most part, Eugene believed, they were girls of arrested emotional development, capable of a dogged and childlike loyalty to anyone who was kind to them. Eugene accepted the fact that a girl could drift into the profession out of helplessness. He met many who told him their histories of a losing struggle to stay alive by respectable standards.

O'Neill first took up the cause of the prostitute in a one-act play called *The Web*, which he wrote in 1913 and whose heroine was a girl named Rose Thomas. Rose is helplessly bound to a pimp named Steve, with whom she lives and who mistreats her and takes all her money. In a state of advanced tuberculosis, Rose would probably have given up trying to stay alive if it were not for her baby, whom she loves, nourishes and protects in the squalid room where Steve keeps her. An escaped gangster who intercedes for her with the brutal Steve asks her:

"Why d'yuh stand fur him anyway? Why don't yuh take the kid and beat it away from him? . . . why don't yuh cut this life and be on the level . . . git a job some place?"

Rose replies: "D'yuh suppose they'd keep me any place if they knew what I was? And d'yuh suppose he wouldn't tell them or have somebody else tell them? Yuh don't know the game I'm up against. I've tried that job thing. I've looked for decent work and I've starved at it. A year after I first hit this town I quit and tried to be on the level. I got a job at housework—workin' twelve hours a day for twenty-five dollars a month. And I worked like a dog, too, and never left the house, I was so scared of seein' some one who knew me. But what was the use? One night they have a guy to dinner who's seen me some place when I was on the town. He tells the lady—his duty he said it was—and she fires me right off the reel. I tried the same thing a lot of times. But there was always some one who'd drag me back. And then I quit tryin'. There didn't seem to be no use. They—all the good people—they got me where I am and they're going to keep me there. Reform? Take it from me it can't be done. They won't let yuh do it, and that's Gawd's truth."

The same sense of being trapped by circumstances is expressed by O'Neill's later heroine, Anna Christie.

—Arthur and Barbara Gelb, *O'Neill* (New York: Harper & Row, 1962): pp. 125–127

TRAVIS BOGARD ON THE DIFFERENCES BETWEEN *CHRIS CHRISTOPHERSON* AND *ANNA CHRISITE*

[Travis Bogard was Professor of English and Dramatic Art and Chairman of Dramatic Art at the University of California, Berkeley, and is the author of *The Tragic Satire of John Webster.* In this selection, Bogard compares O'Neill's earlier version of his story *Chris Christopherson* with *Anna Christie,* focusing on the shift in significance of the characters of Chris and Anna.]

⟨A⟩fter Anna appears, strong in her direction, moving toward self-fulfillment, Chris can no longer hold stage center. His is a character defined by its lack of will, and, therefore, if truly limned, he can take no action. His antagonism to Anna's betrothal to a sailor is part of his chronic hatred of the sea, but even in *Chris* ⟨the original version of Anna Christie⟩, the hatred does not lead to action until a gossiping steward maliciously goads him to attempt murder. His acceptance of the marriage comes as he crouches, strangely passive despite the knife in his hand, and is forced to overhear a long love scene. In its structure, the scene is not unlike Act III of *A Moon for the Misbegotten,* but in its effect, because Chris's action is forced on him, it is the merest melodrama, and Chris is reduced to something less than the obsessed, brooding man O'Neill had known, the man who was ripe only for death. To force him, as O'Neill did at first, to violent, self-determining action is to betray the character.

Not only is Chris reduced to something less than tragic, but Anna and Paul are caught up in an insoluble dilemma.

Paul, like Chris, is a refugee from his destiny. Both men have, in the seaman's phrase, "swallowed the anchor." Paul defines the term as meaning "to loose your grip, to whine and blame something outside yourself for your misfortune, to quit and refuse to fight back any more, to be afraid to take any more chances because you're sure you're no longer strong enough to make things come out right, to shrink from any more effort and be content to anchor fast in the thing you are."

Paul's contentment with the second mate's berth is his weakness. This job, like Chris's barge, is an ethical tideflat. It lies between the responsibility of the officers and the physical labors of the crew. It is a peaceful world where a man, freed of ambition, can follow the drift of his life as a "citizen of the sea." Anna's love, however, fires him, as their marriage moves Chris, into a less phlegmatic pattern of existence, and the play ends rosily.

Andersen's phrase "citizen of the sea" leads to a second important, but conflicting element of theme. Anna, like her later fallen counterpart, has known nothing of the sea. Yet in the fog, drifting on the barge, she talks as Mickey and Devlin talked in the first scene, urging Chris to return to the sea, his proper world. She, unlike her father, has neither fear nor hatred of the sea. If something happens, she feels it will be God's will. To this, Chris cries out in protest: The sea is not God! But as he speaks, the foghorn of the *Londonderry* is heard for the first time, and shortly thereafter, the barge is sunk and Anna has met Paul Andersen. Clearly, although O'Neill has tied a heavy weight to this orthodox love story, the implications are that the sea *is* God, that its way is not to be resisted, and, considering the ending, that its way is good.

Anna and Paul find that they share this identification with the sea, responding to its power as if that response were an inheritance of their blood. They, like all who are the citizens of the sea, belong to the sea and permit her to transmute her energy into will through them. Such "citizens" are necessarily will-less drifters, but their drift is the sea's drift, and their reward is the special sense of elemental belonging which worship of a nameless god makes possible.

Chris Christopherson is a failure because its two central thematic conceptions refuse to merge. Is Andersen, as a "citizen of the sea," to be condemned because he has "swallowed the anchor?" Is it enough to "be long" in total identification with the god, sharing its will-lessness, or must one take arms against the sea and struggle to shape one's destiny? Andersen's resolution is evidently makeshift. In the perspective of Edmund Tyrone's identification with the sea, and the similar sense of "belonging" to some large elemental force which all of O'Neill's heroes seek, Andersen's "citizenship" is not to be denied its value. Yet O'Neill renounces it, and substitutes instead—the year is 1920—a "go-getter," sea-going Babbitt, thus dismissing his earlier conviction of the sea's malignancy with the easiest of compromises—the happy ending, based on self-reform to gain the affection of a pretty girl.

—Travis Bogard, "*Anna Christie:* Her Fall and Rise," *O'Neill: A Collection of Critical Essays,* ed. John Gassner (Englewood Cliffs, NJ: Prentice-Hall, 1964): pp. 66–67

WINIFRED FRAZER ON THE MYTH OF POSEIDON

[Winifred Frazer is the author of *American Drama Between the Wars: A Critical History* and *E. G. and E. G. O: Emma Goldman and The Iceman Cometh.* In this excerpt, Frazer examines "*Anna Christie*" as a Poseidon-like tale of man versus God.]

Eugene O'Neill, more than any other American playwright of his time, had a feeling for myth and its enactment in ritual and drama. Witness his use of masks, his recognition of the power of a syncopated drum beat, his understanding of Oedipal family relationships, his satirical outlook on man's worship of the machine rather than of his essential Dionysian or Appolonian nature, his intuitive feeling for choric responses, his clear portrayal of the life-God Eros and the death-God Thanatos in conflict and collusion, his worship of the earth mother, his awe of the primal father, his feeling for resurrection in both Biblical and pagan mythology, his sense of the timeless and the cyclic, and his comprehension of the rites of passage to manhood.

But perhaps Poseidon presided over his psyche more than any other God. As a young boy, in a widely reproduced photograph, he gazes winsomely to sea from his seat on a large rock near the O'Neill's New London waterfront home. And the last house the dying playwright owned was at Marblehead on the rocky Massachusetts coast, where the eye had a vast wide-angle view of the Atlantic Ocean and the ear was assaulted by the battering of the waves against the concrete sea wall below the house. In between, O'Neill lived on the sand dunes at the tip of Cape Cod in a remodeled Coast Guard Station which the waves eventually carried into the sea, and in a mansion-sized "cottage" on the Georgia coast at Sea Island, where the sea was murky and warm. His sea voyages in the years 1910 and 1911 to Argentina, Africa, and England affected him deeply. According to the Gelbs, he learned to stand watch on the highest yardarms and found it the most exalting experience of his life. Also, the only physical activity he seems to have enjoyed was swimming—which he could do for long distances far from shore in icy water. ⟨. . .⟩

⟨T⟩he fate which the Gods mete out ⟨in *Anna Christie*⟩ is inevitable. Larry, the bartender, in the play's opening scene, listens skeptically to Chris's denunciation of the sea and his tale of protecting his daughter from its malevolent influence through her inland upbringing. "This girl, now," he prophesies, "'ll be marryin' a sailor herself, likely. It's in the blood." Generations of sea-faring men cannot produce a daughter who is not attracted to it. As surely as the Mannons are cursed by their Fate as New England Puritans, so are the Christophersons by the Sea. Chris's ardent hope that Anna will marry some "good, steady land fallar here in East" is obviously not in the cards. In fact Chris himself belies the wish by singing in expectation of that happy event. "My Yosephine, come board the ship,"—a most unlikely song for a "land fallar."

When Anna enters, she intimates that the open sea is the world for her by revealing that she "never could stand being caged up nowheres." The fate of the characters is thus exposed in the opening scene and as in Greek Tragedy the play consists of its unfolding. Old Marthy, in spite of her admiration for Chris, does agree that he is nutty on the one point of avoiding the sea and bursts into "hoarse, ironical laughter" when she learns that it is living on a farm that has made Anna a prostitute. But when Chris later learns the truth, far from seeing the irony, *he* attributes her fall in some mysterious way to the old devil sea. And he is perhaps not far wrong, for although she first exclaims, "Me? On a dirty coal barge! What do you think I am?" and Larry also exclaims, "On a coal barge! She'll not like that, I'm thinkin'" still it turns out that Anna experiences a magical transformation under the Sea God's spell.

> It's like I'd come home after a long visit away some place. It all seems like I'd been here before lots of times—on boats. . . . Feel so—so—like I'd found something I'd missed and been

looking for—'s if this was the right place for me to fit in. . . .
I feel clean. . . . And I feel happy for once.

Chris has forebodings, but Anna chides him for his fear that he is a fool for having brought her on the voyage and comments satirically that whatever happens is God's will. Chris "starts to his feet with fierce protests," shouting, "dat ole davil sea, she ain't God."

—Winifred L. Frazer, "Chris and Poseidon: Man Versus God in *Anna Christie* (1969)," *The Critical Response to Eugene O'Neill,* ed. John H. Houchin (Westport, CT: Greenwood Press, 1993): pp. 30–32

FREDERIC I. CARPENTER ON REALISM AND ROMANTICISM

[Frederic I. Carpenter is the author of *Emerson and Asia* (1930), *Emerson Handbook* (1953), *American Literature and the Dream* (1955), *Robinson Jeffers* (1962), and *Laurens van der Post* (1969). He a lecturer at the University of Chicago, Harvard University, and the University of California at Berkley. In this excerpt, Carpenter discusses the characters' realism and romanticism in *Anna Christie*.]

The character of Chris, "childishly self-willed and weak, of an obstinate kindliness," is one of O'Neill's minor triumphs. Without any understanding of himself and without any realistic love or responsibility for this daughter whom he has never seen for fifteen years, he yet imagines that merely by shielding her from the sea he can protect her. In his "obstinate kindliness" he seems the perfect foil for the earlier "emperor" Jones, with his equally obstinate worldliness. But the character of Mat Burke, at the other extreme, is that of a romantic Irishman whose primitive innocence and blind love for Anna never seem quite credible. The romantic unreality of Mat weakens the play.

Between the realistic Chris and the unrealistic Mat stands Anna Christie. Unlike Chris, her character had developed very slowly in O'Neill's imagination; but, unlike that of Mat, it is now fully realized. Its complexity foreshadows the later characters of O'Neill's major plays, who seem both realistic and archetypal. Moreover, Anna is that typical figure of modern literature—the prostitute with a heart of gold. She possesses a clear intelligence which sees through the childish illusions of her father, and a perfect integrity which will not let her deceive her lover. Like Dostoevski's ideal prostitute in *Crime and Punishment,* Anna seems to stand above the sordid world and to become an instrument for its salvation. Also like Dostoevski's heroine, she has been called "sentimental." Why should a girl so pure in heart have taken to prostitution in the first place?

The character of Anna is crucial. She is drawn from life, but is larger than life. Like Dostoevski, O'Neill knew his prostitutes: her speech and her mannerisms are wholly convincing. And the actual details of her regeneration from the effects of her past are copied from letters of the former mistress of O'Neill's best friend, Terry Carlin. But beyond this, the deeper motivation of Anna's prostitution is derived from O'Neill's own psychological experience. Her childhood neglect by her father, her loneliness in alien surroundings, her seduction by a relative, and her drifting into prostitution—all reflect O'Neill's own feeling of desertion by his own parents, his loneliness at boarding school, the influence of his own brother, and the resulting profligacy of his own youth. The central theme of the play is the irresponsibility of Anna's father, which for a time drove the heroine into prostitution, but it did not destroy her.

Like the character of Anna, the ending of the play has been criticized for its mixed nature. It is not tragic, but it is true to life. Replying to criticism, O'Neill wrote: "It would have been so obvious and easy . . . to have made my last act a tragic one. It could have been done in ten different ways. . . . But looking deep into the hearts of my people, I saw that . . . they would act in just the silly, immature, compromising way that I have made them act." The play is not a tragedy, and should not be damned for its "failure" as one. Like the later *Strange Interlude,* it is a serious study of modern life, which dramatizes that mixture of comedy and tragedy most characteristic of life. Even for O'Neill, life was not always pure tragedy.

—Frederic I. Carpenter, *Eugene O'Neill* (Boston: G. K. Hall and Co., 1979): pp. 92–93

JAMES A. ROBINSON ON THE RELIGIOUS UNDERTONES IN *ANNA CHRISTIE*

[James A. Robinson is a professor of English at the University of Maryland. His articles on O'Neill, Arthur Miller, Sam Shepard, and Edith Wharton have appeared in journals such as *Comparative Drama, Markham Review* and *Modern Drama*. In this excerpt, Robinson discusses the personification of the sea and the religious significance of *Anna Christie*.]

"*Anna Christie*" resembles *The Moon of the Caribbees* in two major respects. First, while it exhibits some naturalistic sensationalism—drunkenness, violence, and prostitution—its meaning is fundamentally religious. O'Neill declared "the big underlying idea of the sea" as central to the dramatic action, so the spirit of the sea once again emerges as the true protagonist. The second similarity involves the subordination of plot to other dramatic elements. In *Caribbees*, atmosphere prevails; in "*Anna Christie*," characterization is paramount. Writing to his agent about cuts in the Philadelphia production of *Chris Christopherson* (which later was revised into "*Anna Christie*"), O'Neill complained that "you can't cut a play in which the whole plot is a study in character built up bit by bit down to bare essentials of story without losing your play in the process." Nine days later, he reluctantly conceded that "such cutting might have been justified," but still lamented that "my character sketch [of Chris] must have gone to hell in the process." Ironically, though, when he reworked the play, the main character was no longer the barge captain Chris, but his daughter—the young woman nicknamed "Anna Christie."

How had Anna—originally a respectable typist with a subordinate role—been transformed into a sentimentalized prostitute who stole the spotlight from her father? The answer lies in the play's focus on the sea. "The sea is a woman to me," O'Neill once wrote Carlotta, and this notion eventually advanced to center stage in the person of Anna, worshipper and representative of the sea. As in *Caribbees*, then, one character reproduces the sea on stage. But the sea god of "Anna Christie" contains more facets than the mysterious force behind *Caribbees*. While *Anna* perceives an ironic life force shaping man's destiny, its plot draws more heavily on Greek tragedy than do the earlier sea plays. Christianity also looms larger in *Anna,* for the sea symbolically baptizes and redeems the heroine. Most important, the play's god is more Oriental in detail than that of *Caribbees.* Enveloping the characters in its fog, the sea unifies reality and blurs distinctions between personalities; and like Brahman in the state of māyā it also misleads everyone, and defies our relativistic notions of good and evil.

Perhaps the most obvious source of *Anna* is classical Greek tragedy, with its sense of antagonism between man and the gods. A family curse, emanating from the sea, seems to lie on the Christopherson clan. Chris's father, brothers and son have all left home to become sailors and nearly all have died on the water. ⟨. . .⟩ Her father, though, views all this as one more ironic trick of "dat ole davil," which dooms Anna to the same misery as everyone else in his family. His fears are quickly confirmed. In a final twist of fate, Chris and his detested prospective son-in-law are scheduled to sail off together on the *Londonderry* for a year, thereby deserting Anna—and subjecting her to the same loneliness suffered by all the Christopherson women.

Curiously, the play treats Chris's fatalism ambiguously. Anna considers him a weakling who rationalizes his past unwillingness to care for her by pointing his finger at the sea. She reacts *"with a trace of scorn in her voice"* to his excuses, asking skeptically, "then you think the sea's to blame for everything, eh?" Moreover, the traditionally comic denouement—two lovers about to marry over a father's objections—makes the old man's gloom seem out of place. O'Neill himself, however, implicitly sided with Chris, in a letter to the *New York Times* about the misinterpretation of the conclusion as a contrived happy ending: "I wanted to have the audience leave with a deep feeling of life flowing on, of the past which is never the past—but always the birth of the future—of a problem solved for the moment but by the very nature of its solution involving new problems." As he observes, in the final scene all three characters intuit a mysterious fate at work. Burke has *"superstitious premonitions"* about shipping out with Chris; Anna is heard *"forcing a laugh"* to try to break the spell; Chris's final words call our attention to the "fog, fog, fog, all bloody time! You can't see vhere you vas going, no. Only dat ole davil sea—she knows!" The dialogue and setting thus dramatize the helpless subjection of all three to a larger force. And in its dominance the sea both parallels the fate of Greek tragedy, and more broadly expresses the dualistic Western distrust of nature.

The sea's portrait is also informed by another Western tradition, Christianity. Anna washes away her sins and feels reborn: "I seem to have forgot—everything that's happened—like it didn't matter no more. And I feel clean, somehow—like you feel yust after you've took a bath." The sea soon washes up Matt, providing Anna an opportunity for love that purifies her even more.

—James A. Robinson, *Eugene O'Neill and Oriental Thought: A Divided Vision* (Carbondale and Edwardsville: Southern Illinois University Press, 1982): pp. 94–96

VIRGINIA FLOYD ON O'NEILL'S DEPICTION OF ANNA

[Virginia Floyd is the editor of *Eugene O'Neill: The Unfinished Plays; Eugene O'Neill: A World View;* and *O'Neill: A New Assessment.* She was also a professor of English at Bryant College for many years. In this excerpt, Floyd discusses the character of Anna, particularly O'Neill's early conception of her in *Chris Christopherson.*]

Anna is more seriously flawed dramatically than Chris in the early version ⟨of *Chris Christopherson,*⟩ precisely because she was conceived of as flawless. The author depicts her as perfect physically and morally, a doll figure rather than a realistic flesh-and-blood woman, unlike any other female he had portrayed before or, possibly, had ever met. Agnes Boulton describes her husband's efforts in the winter and spring of 1919 to breathe life into his aloof heroine and to make her convincing. She states: "I used to secretly wonder how old Chris had ever come to have such a daughter. She didn't like herself either, it seems, and even then was secretly rebelling and a year or so later became a prostitute."

The early concept of Anna, the perfect woman, is the antithesis of the tough, cynical prostitute in the first act of *Anna Christie*. The author, unfortunately, attempts to merge the two Annas in later acts.

Little effort is made to motivate her conversion, her sudden emergence as a purified woman, which is attributed vaguely to the sea in Act II and to love in Act IV. The strong, cynical side asserts itself briefly in the third act when she firmly denounces her father and lover, but the toughness dissolves into all-forgiving penitence in the last act.

O'Neill's difficulty in creating a credible Anna stems perhaps from the fact that the Swedish heroine was an imaginary figure. His portraits of Chris and the characters at Johnny the Priest's are true-to-life, perhaps because he had simply to evoke them from memory. His wife, Agnes, states, "Old Chris—how real *he* was! It was Chris Gene really knew and loved, and old Marthy too—and the bums and outcasts in the first act down at Johnny the Priest's saloon on South Street in lower New York."

The second, and equally serious, weakness of *Anna Christie,* deriving probably from its uncertain characterization, is its plot. The change of title, from *Chris Christopherson* to *Anna Christie,* signifies the shift in focus sought by the author. The emphasis of the former play was Chris and his relationship with his daughter; that of the latter, Anna's inner conflict and destiny. The father-daughter clash becomes a minor theme. Both plots seem faulty at the core. O'Neill creates a flawed tragic heroine and two complex secondary male figures, all held captive to an avenging sea by their superstitions and premonitions. Trapped by the inevitability of fate and their own natures, the three are doomed to tragedy.

Yet O'Neill gives the play a contradictory happy ending. In a letter in 1920 to George Jean Nathan, he suggests that audiences look beyond the final reconciliation of Mat and Anna to the brooding sea that seethes outside. "The happy ending is merely a comma at the end of a gaudy introductory clause, with the body of the sentence unwritten," O'Neill remarks. "In fact, I once thought of calling the play *Comma*." He concludes by saying: "all of them at the end have a vague foreboding that although they have had their moment, the decision still rests with the sea which has achieved the conquest of Anna."

The makeshift happy ending haunted the author for years. On May 8, 1932, he wrote to Langner, suggesting that the Theatre Guild revive *Anna Christie* with "the last act played as I obviously intended in the writing not the conventional happy ending as directed by Hoppy—I could heighten to sea-fog-fate uncertainty atmosphere by slight cutting and rewriting." In the Nathan letter he speaks of "the trappings of theatre" inhibiting "sincerity of life," the necessities of plot influencing characterization. When he began the two-year period devoted to *Chris Christopherson—Anna Christie*, O'Neill had not developed the skill to manipulate the intricacies of plot while sustaining believably motivated characters. The 1920s would see this integration. O'Neill gave the world a flawed *Anna Christie*, but it is one of his most interesting failures.

—Virginia Floyd, *The Plays of Eugene O'Neill: A New Assessment* (New York: Frederick Ungar Publishing Company, 1985): pp. 199–201

RONALD H. WAINSCOTT ON LANGUAGE, THEME, AND THE STAGING OF *ANNA CHRISTIE*

[Ronald H. Wainscott has been Associate Professor and Director of Graduate Studies at Indiana University since 1995. He is a National Endowment for the Humanities Fellow and a multiple grant recipient. Dr. Wainscott has written numerous articles, chapters, and entries for such publications as *The Cambridge History of American Theatre* and *The Cambridge Companion to Eugene O'Neill.* He is the author of two books, *The Emergence of the Modern American Theater, 1914–1929* (1997); and *Staging O'Neill: The Experimental Years, 1920–1934* (1988), from which this extract is taken.]

About one year before the October rehearsals of *Anna Christie,* O'Neill was very enthusiastic as he completed a severe revision of *Chris Christopherson* and retitled it *The Ole Davil.* He resubmitted his play in November to Tyler, who was not interested in a second solo attempt with this material. By the time Hopkins ⟨the director⟩, received the play in early summer after more changes, it had its final title, which signaled a significant shift in focus away from Chris to his daughter, Anna Christopherson. The revision not only refocused the material but significantly altered the scenic requirements. O'Neill eliminated the barge wreck and extracted all three steamer settings which scenically had cluttered *Chris*.

Centering on a sympathetically presented fallen woman, this play would later be called by O'Neill his "most conventional" work, "although its subject matter was damned unconventional in our theatre of 1921." Of course, the fallen woman was a very old device used extensively in much melodrama and realism long before O'Neill. It was in his manner of presentation, however, that O'Neill was experimenting. The playwright not only gave rugged language to Anna and the waterfront characters but also created explicit situations and revelations, especially in acts I and III.

Not surprisingly, this play attracted many curious sensation seekers who came to be shocked or titillated by language and situation, just as they flocked to the sex farce *The Demi-Virgin* by Avery Hopwood at the same time. Gilbert Seldes, for example, who saw the second performance of *Anna Christie*, exclaimed, "Destroy the audience!" He lamented that "every time Anna Christie spoke the vicious racy ugly slang of her past, every word of which should have fallen like sleet upon our stricken hearts, the audience of which I was a part gathered itself with refreshment and laughed." Seldes' experience was not an aberration. Percy Hammond, who reviewed opening night but returned for four subsequent performances, complained that although Hopkins' actors delivered the material very seriously, each audience laughed frequently at the harsh language. This situation became an ongoing problem in the 1920s for several of O'Neill's directors who attempted to address rough language and sensitive social situations without catering to sensation-seeking audiences which so often gravitated to O'Neill's plays. The difficulty was especially evident in *The Hairy Ape, All God's Chillun Got Wings,* and *Desire Under the Elms*.

More troublesome to O'Neill at the time, however, was a subtle experiment which failed in his own estimation but which, like the language and dramatic situations, may have contributed to the commercial success of the play. Many months before production O'Neill sent a copy of *Anna Christie* to George Jean Nathan. The critic's major criticism of the play was its apparent happy ending. O'Neill took umbrage at this and insisted that the audience was meant to infer that the future for Anna and Mat was at best uncertain and probably arduous. In O'Neill's view the audience should sense that the play does not have a storybook finale.

O'Neill did not act on Nathan's warning, and numerous critics of the production referred to the happy ending; several, such as Towse, De Foe, and Woollcott, objected to it as a contrivance. The *Sun* wondered if O'Neill was "gradually degenerating into a Broadway playwright." O'Neill privately attacked everyone's obtuseness ("either I am crazy, or they all are"), but with more restraint explained in print what the audience was meant to discern: "In the last few minutes . . . I tried to show that dramatic gathering of new forces out of the old. I wanted to have the audience leave with a deep feeling . . . of a problem solved for the moment but by the very nature of its solution involving new problems." As published, the inconclusive ending which O'Neill sought is subtly implied, but not strongly enough to negate the obvious optimism of Anna and Mat. In production, however, Hopkins intended or allowed the final cheerful mood to dominate. Nevertheless, Woollcott's assessment of the production's conclusion suggests at least part of what O'Neill was seeking: "There is probably no end of misery for everybody [the characters] hidden just ahead in the enfolding mists of the sea. It is a happy ending with the author's fingers crossed." Although in 1932 O'Neill tried to blame Hopkins for directing it as a "conventional happy ending," neither playwright nor director had stressed a problematic future for Anna. "I must have failed in this attempt" was O'Neill's public admission in 1921.

—Ronald H. Wainscott, *Staging O'Neill: The Experimental Years, 1920–1934* (New Haven: Yale University Press, 1988): pp. 80–82

Plot Summary of
The Iceman Cometh

Eugene O'Neill may have explained the central theme of *The Iceman Cometh* when he said, "There is always one dream left, one final dream, no matter how low you have fallen, down there at the bottom of the bottle. I know, because I saw it." What O'Neill had also seen at the two primary haunts of his youth—bars named "the Hell-Hole" and "Jimmy the Priest's"—were the basic figures for the characters in *The Iceman Cometh*. The philosophical Larry Slade is O'Neill's surrogate. Harry Hope's saloon and boarding house, according to Larry, is "the No Chance Saloon. It's Bedrock Bar, The End of the Line Café, The Bottom of the Sea Rathskeller!" The group of men and women who inhabit Harry Hope's "cheap ginmill" are those who have nothing to do and nowhere else to go. It is the last refuge for a desperate crew whose alcoholism has become a sort of faith. Without it, their illusions disintegrate and only the grim truth is left. And as they discover, that truth cannot sustain them. As Larry says early in the first act, "To hell with the truth! As history of the world proves, the truth has no bearing on anything. It's irrelevant and immaterial, as the lawyers say. The lie of a pipe dream is what gives life to the whole misbegotten mad lot of us, drunk or sober."

The Iceman Cometh is primarily a character study and an exploration of the fundamental role that illusions—"pipe dreams"—play in people's lives. The plot of *The Iceman Cometh* centers around the annual visit of a hardware salesman, Theodore Hickman, or "Hickey," to Harry Hope's saloon on the proprietor's birthday. Hickey's appearance begins a ritual in which the former inhabitant of Harry Hope's funds an extended drunken celebration, which includes all of Harry's regulars and roomers and lasts for days.

Although Hickey's arrival is always eagerly anticipated, this year, on Harry's 60th birthday, the salesman seems greatly changed. Normally jovial and easygoing, he now behaves as a prophet of reform. His message is that everyone must face the truth about himself or herself, no matter how harsh it may be. He implores his friends to forsake their illusions and their promises to amend their lives "tomorrow," to look at themselves honestly regardless of how painful it is. He tries to expose each character's pipe dream, and through constant badgering, urges every one of them to face reality by leaving the saloon and ending their dependence on Harry Hope's alcohol.

Though Hickey is the impetus for the play's main action, Larry Slade is a more central character. A former member of the anarchist movement, Larry is a disillusioned wise man and the "commentator" at the saloon. He observes and analyzes, but he does not act. Declaring that he is condemned to see both sides of every issue, he refuses to choose a course of action, or even to give advice on taking action. A man who has fallen from faith and privilege into the world of the most dispossessed, Larry poses as the detached truth-seeker among those on the lowest social rungs; in reality, he is as paralyzed with inaction as they are.

Parallels of the playwright's life can be seen in Larry's biography: his youthful idealism, which led him to join the anarchist movement, his consequent rejection of the movement as yet another vehicle for greed and personal gain. When Don Parritt seeks out the boarder in the **Act I**, Larry is wary of the boy and shows no compassion for what he views as a reminder of his previous life. (Don is the son of Rosa Parritt, one of the great leaders of the movement and a former lover of Larry's.) Moreover, Don's moral predicament seems unsolvable to Larry; the boy is drowning in a sea of guilt over having betrayed his mother.

Hickey's arrival defers action between Larry and Don Parritt. Larry is very suspicious of Hickey's changed behavior. Unlike most of the other characters, who make vain attempts at complying with Hickey's heartfelt wishes that they find peace, Larry remains detached, an "objective" viewer of the reforms Hickey tries to make. Nearly obsessed with his project to crush the pipe dreams of the other characters, Hickey's motivation does not surface immediately. When the truth of his life emerges, however, he is revealed as a horrifying example of his own philosophy of truth-telling. In the end, his ardent message of reform, delivered over the course of three acts, rings hollow. His own seeming rehabilitation is a cover for a devastating and irreversible truth.

We learn during the course of the play that Hickey's wife has been a profound source of guilt for him. Stalwart in her love, she repeatedly forgives his drunken binges and many infidelities. But her faithfulness is a painful reminder of Hickey's inadequacy; instead of telling the truth about her, he has routinely joked about her ongoing affair with "the iceman."

When Hickey reveals at the end of **Act II** that his wife is dead, the other characters interpret his reformation as the by-product of grief. His response is premonitory: "I've got to feel glad, for her sake," he says, "Because she's at peace. She's rid of me at last. Hell, I don't have to tell you—you all know what I was like. You can imagine what she went through, married to a no-good cheater and drunk like I was. And there was no way out of it for her. Because she loved me." Only in **Act III** do we learn that Hickey's wife was murdered.

In a setting in which each character seems badly in need of salvation of some sort, Hickey at first appears both moral and reasonable in his effort to reform his friends. Though he badgers them and is cruel at times, he is often forgiven because his intentions seem well-placed, and because he is supposedly grieving. His affection for them seems genuine and his mission honorable. But the truth that Hickey lays claim to is a lie.

Act IV exposes Hickey's startling confession—unable to bear his wife's unerring faith in him, he kills her to "give her peace." Suicide was not an alternative, he explains; his death would only have increased her anguish. Hickey's intricate rationalization of his actions reveals a mind far more deeply disturbed and rooted in unreality than that of any of the other characters. His wife's pipe dream—and her undoing—was her belief that Hickey would eventually mend his ways.

Yet Hickey has by this time reported himself to the police, and two detectives arrive at the saloon in time to hear his full confession to his friends. In a brief outburst, Hickey reveals his true feelings toward his wife, admitting that he killed her not only so that she'd be free "from the misery of loving me," but also so that he would be freed from her love: "I saw it meant peace for me, too," he says, "I felt as though a ton of guilt was lifted off my mind. I remember I stood by the bed and suddenly I had to laugh. . . . I remember I heard myself speaking to her, as if it was something I'd always wanted to say: 'Well, you know what you can do with your pipe dream now, you damned bitch!'"

The ultimate irony of the play is that Hickey's admission of hatred is the truth, but he cannot face it. If he did say those words, he protests, then he must have been insane. The other characters, in true form, agree with him—insanity is the only acceptable answer for Hickey's behavior. His friends allow him his final pipe dream. Unlike him, they know that he needs it to survive. "Every one of us noticed he was nutty the minute he showed up here!" Harry Hope tells the policemen. "Bejees, if you'd heard all the crazy bull he was pulling about bringing us peace—like a bughouse preacher escaped from an asylum!"

Harry's declaration seems to free the saloon regulars from Hickey's suffocating self-righteousness, giving them a forlorn sense of hope. Hickey, however, has nothing left. "Do you suppose I give a damn about life now?" he asks the policemen as they lead him away. "Why, you bonehead, I haven't got a single damned lying hope or pipe dream left!"

The drama of Hickey's confession once again spurs Don Parritt's desperate attempt to elicit sympathy from Larry Slade for having betrayed his mother. Parritt views Hickey as lucky because "It's all decided for him. I wish it was decided for me. I've never been any good at deciding things. Even about selling out, it was the tart the detective agency got after me who put it in my mind [to turn my mother in]." In anguish, Larry, who claims he is doomed to see both sides of every issue, makes a decision for Parritt. "Go! Get the hell out of life, God damn you, before I choke it out of you!" he cries. Parritt thanks Larry for understanding, and he exits.

While the other characters, who are revisiting their familiar pipe dreams, are talking, Larry waits for the sound that tells him that Parritt has committed suicide by jumping off the top of the building. In the final moments of the play, the newly revived drinkers break into a cacophony of singing, oblivious to what has just happened. Larry is left in his own poisonous solitude, and as the play ends he proclaims himself converted to Hickey's religion—the religion of death. ❈

List of Characters in
The Iceman Cometh

Harry Hope is the proprietor of the run-down saloon and boarding house where the play takes place. A gruff, generous, and volatile man who frequently threatens to revoke credit and evict tenants, Harry does neither because he not only sympathizes with his friends, but he also identifies with them. He has not left his building in the 20 years since the death of his wife, Bess, but he often talks about "taking a walk around the ward." He has become very much like his tenants and customers, who rarely have reason to leave the bar.

Larry Slade is the resident philosopher of Harry Hope's saloon and a boarder in his rooming house. His life has reached its low point as part of Hope's "family," yet he feels somehow comforted by the fact that he cannot sink any lower. In his youth, he was an idealist and a member of the Anarchist movement, until he became disillusioned and abandoned the movement. A former lover of Rosa Parritt, he was once viewed as a surrogate father by her son, Don Parritt.

Theodore Hickman ("**Hickey**") is a hardware salesman who returns to the saloon each year on Harry's birthday to sponsor a drunken celebration that lasts for days. This year, however, he is sober, and he badgers the other characters to follow his lead, stop drinking, and carry out their "pipe dreams." The reason behind his changed behavior forms the climax of the play.

Don Parritt is a new roomer at Harry's. He is the son of an infamous anarchist, Rosa Parritt, who has been imprisoned for her involvement in a terrorist attack. He has gone into hiding because of his family name, and as the play progresses we learn that he is responsible for the arrest of his mother and her friends. He suffers intractable guilt over his betrayal and discovers that in trying to escape his mother's fanaticism, he has become trapped in a different way.

James Cameron ("**Jimmy Tomorrow**") is a former journalist who covered the Boer War and a roomer at Harry's. He earned his nickname from his constant vow to get his affairs in order and get his old job back "tomorrow."

Hugo Kalmar was once an editor of Anarchist periodicals. A tenant at Harry's, he is either sleeping or passed out throughout much of the play, rousing himself occasionally to sing a French ditty or utter meaningless epithets against his companions.

Cecil Lewis ("the Captain"), a former captain in the British infantry and one of Harry Hope's tenants.

Pat McGloin, a roomer at Harry's and a sidekick of Ed Mosher, is a former police lieutenant who was presumably thrown off the force for grafting.

Ed Mosher is Harry Hope's brother-in-law, the brother of Bess. He is a con man and former employee of a traveling circus.

Joe Mott, the only black character in the play, was once the proprietor of a Negro gambling house. Harry used his influence to see that Joe was not harassed by police raids.

Willie Oban is a Harvard Law School alumnus who is a few decades younger than most of the men who room at Harry's. Although he tells others that he was a "brilliant student," he never tried a case.

Piet Wetjoen ("the General") is a former leader of a Boer commando and one of Harry Hope's tenants. He is constantly involved in good-natured verbal skirmishes with Cecil Lewis.

Rocky Pioggi is the tough but good-natured night bartender and a roomer at Harry's. He is a also a pimp for Pearl and Margie, although he does not see himself as such because he has a "regular job."

Chuck Morello is the day bartender and a roomer at Harry's.

Pearl and **Margie** are streetwalkers and roomers at Harry's. They are "managed" by Rocky, the night bartender of Harry's saloon.

Cora is a streetwalker and the girlfriend of Chuck.

Moran and **Lieb** are policemen who arrest Hickey. ❀

Critical Views on
The Iceman Cometh

EDWIN A. ENGEL ON LARRY SLADE AS PHILOSOPHER

[Edwin A. Engel is a theater critic and lecturer at Harvard University. In this excerpt, Engel examines the character of Larry Slade, theorizing that Larry's "pipe dreams" are feelings of faith and love that have taken a wrong turn.]

It is characteristic of Larry that he has never been able to make a choice, even a less crucial one than that which he now faces. His indecision, as he sees it, has stemmed not from sinful skepticism but from a more virtuous source: from tolerance and compassion. "Life is too much for me," he wails. "I'll be a weak fool looking with pity at the two sides of everything till the day I die!" Here, it seems that Larry is merely trying to cheer himself up. For most of the time there is less virtue in his incertitude than obfuscation. Thus he complains that he "was born condemned to see all sides of a question. When you're born like that," he points out, "the questions multiply for you until in the end it's all question and no answer." Although O'Neill created Larry in the midst of world catastrophe—between 1939 and 1946—he endowed his wise old character with a singular lack of perspicacity, with a curious deficiency of moral sense. Obsessed with his own problems the playwright was unable to immerse himself in the contemplation of external disaster. Consequently Larry's vision of evil is as narrow, his insight as shallow as John Loving's. Like the hero of *Days Without End*, he bitterly denounces a suffering, foundering mankind for its stupidity and greed, and announces his secession:

> All I know is I'm sick of life! I'm through! I've forgotten myself! I'm drowned and contented on the bottom of a bottle. Honor or dishonor, faith or treachery are nothing to me but the opposites of the same stupidity which is ruler and king of life, and in the end they rot into dust in the same grave. All things are the same meaningless joke to me, for they grin at me from the one skull of death.

Having witnessed the "stupid greed of the human circus," Larry has concluded that

> men didn't want to be saved from themselves, for that
> would mean they'd have to give up greed, and they'll never
> pay that price for liberty. So I said to the world, God bless
> all here, and may the best man win and die of gluttony!

In the matter of truth Larry again concurs with the pre-regenerate John Loving: "To hell with the truth!" he exclaims. "As the history of the world proves, the truth has no bearing on anything. It's irrelevant and immaterial, as the lawyers say."

Larry's bitterness is intensified as the play progresses, and the disparity between that emotion and the facts which O'Neill gave to account for it is widened. Larry continues to be a mysterious figure even after we supplement the inadequate facts with inferences. Never completely divulged, the content of his pipe dreams is insufficient motive and cue to his acrimonious expressions of self-loathing, misanthropy, nihilism. Larry is increasingly distressed as certain other characters in the play try to disinter his "dead and buried" dreams. During these attempts, although their outline is dim, we can discern that they were pipe dreams of faith and love. In one instance were it not for the author's interpolation the significance of a remark would go unnoticed. For when, near the end of the play, Larry, moved by horrified pity mumbles, "God rest his soul in peace," O'Neill informed the reader of the play that *a long-forgotten faith* [has returned to Larry] *for a moment* . . . Having called attention to the phenomenon, O'Neill never again referred to it. What spiritual trauma was responsible for the disaffection remains hidden. We are left to deduce that the cause lay in Larry's innate weakness, his compulsion "to see all sides of a question." And it was that weakness in part which led Larry to withdraw from another faith, the Syndicalist-Anarchist Movement. But we infer from information slowly, obliquely conveyed that the situation was complicated by another factor, that of love.

In the course of two days Larry completes a cycle which begins with dubious peace, moves through emotional turmoil, and returns to a peace that is more genuine, the kind which death alone can bring. The turmoil is precipitated by the arrival of two characters: Hickey, a hardware salesman, and Don Parritt, until recently a member of the Movement and son of the woman with whom Larry seems to have been in love. The mission of the former is to sell the derelicts the idea that they can find peace only if they rid themselves of their "lying pipe dreams." Larry alone has perceived that this is the peace of death. Hickey succeeds in persuading some fifteen of the vagrants to make an effort to abandon their dreams, to accept reality and adapt themselves to it. The ensuing commotion of confession, self-revelation, resolution, action provides a spectacle so ridiculous, pitiful, horrifying, and sordid as to justify Larry's denial of love and life, and affirmation of hate and death. Out of the unmasking, one truth, together with its corollary, emerges above all others: love is an illusion, and all women are bitches or whores. Palpable and undisguised symbols of this truth are the three prostitutes, the only women to appear on stage. Yet the presence of four others is felt: Hickey's wife, Evelyn; Parritt's mother, Rosa; Hope's wife, Bessie; Jimmy Cameron's wife, Marjorie. And their stories form the main substance of a weird and discordant symphony. Throughout most of the long piece the tales of Hickey and of Parritt are counterpointed, those of Hope and of Jimmy serving as variations on the main theme. Meanwhile the revelations of the numerous other characters furnish minor background melodies. It is the lesser figures who, as the fourth movement draws to a close, bring the composition to its conclusion in a cacophony of noisy song, laughter, howls, and jeers.

—Edwin A. Engel, *The Haunted Heroes of Eugene O'Neill* (Cambridge, MA: Harvard University Press, 1953): pp. 284–286

ERIC BENTLEY ON STRUCTURE AND DIALOGUE

[Eric Bentley is a literary critic, translator, and writer on the theater. From 1953 to 1969, he was the Brandes-Matthews Professor of Dramatic Literature at Columbia University in New York. He has published numerous dramatic and critical works, including *The Recantation of Galileo Galilei, The Playwright as Thinker, In Search of Theatre,* and *The Theatre of Commitment.* He was editor and translator of *Seven Plays by Bertolt Brecht* and *Naked Masks by Pirandello.* In this excerpt, Bentley compares O'Neill's strict theatrical form and the looseness of his dialogue in *The Iceman Cometh.*]

True, ⟨O'Neill⟩ is a man of the theater and, true, he is an eloquent writer composing, as his colleagues on Broadway usually do not, under the hard compulsion of something he has to say. But his gifts are mutually frustrating. His sense of theatrical form is frustrated by an eloquence that decays into mere repetitious garrulousness. His eloquence is frustrated by the extreme rigidity of the theatrical mold into which it is poured—jelly in an iron jar. Iron. Study, for example, the stage directions of *The Iceman,* and you will see how carefully O'Neill has drawn his ground plan. There everyone sits—a row of a dozen and a half men. And as they sit, the plot progresses; as each new stage is reached, the bell rings, and the curtain comes down. Jelly. Within the tyrannically, mechanically rigid scenes, there is an excessive amount of freedom. The order of speeches can be juggled without loss, and almost any speech can be cut in half.

The eloquence might of course be regarded as clothing that is necessary to cover a much too mechanical man. Certainly, though we gained more by abridging the play than we lost, the abridgment did call attention rather cruelly to the excessively schematic character of the play. Everything is contrived, *voulu,* drawn on the blackboard, thought out beforehand, imposed on the material by the dead hand of calculation. We had started out from the realization that the most lifeless schemata in this overschematic play are the expressionistic ones, but we had been too sanguine in hoping to conceal or cancel them. They are foreshadowed already in the table groupings of Act I (as specified in O'Neill's stage directions). They hold the last act in a death grip. Larry and Parritt are on one side shouting their duet. Hickey is in the center singing his solo. And at the right, arranged en bloc, is everyone else, chanting their comments in what O'Neill himself calls a "chorus."

It would perhaps be churlish to press the point, were O'Neill's ambition in this last act not symptomatic both of his whole endeavor as a playwright and of the endeavor of many other serious playwrights in our time. It is the ambition to transcend realism. O'Neill spoke of it nearly thirty years ago in a program note on Strindberg:

> It is only by means of some form of "super-naturalism" that we may express in the theatre what we comprehend intuitively of that self-obsession which is the particular discount we moderns have to pay for the loan of life. The

old naturalism—or realism if you will (I wish to God some genius were gigantic enough to define clearly the separateness of these terms once and for all!)—no longer applies. It represents our fathers' daring aspirations towards self-recognition by holding the family kodak up to ill-nature. But to us their audacity is blague, we have taken too many snapshots of each other in every graceless position. We have endured too much from the banality of surfaces.

So far, so good. This is a warning against that extreme and narrow form of realism generally known as naturalism. Everyone agrees. The mistake is to talk as if it followed that one must get away from realism altogether, a mistake repeated by every poetaster who thinks can rise above Ibsen by writing flowerily (for example, Christopher Fry as quoted and endorsed by *Time*). Wherever O'Neill tries to clarify his non-realistic theory the only thing that is clear is lack of clarity. For example:

> It was far from my idea in writing *The Great God Brown* that the background pattern of conflicting tides in the soul of man should ever overshadow and thus throw out of proportion the living drama of the recognizable human beings. . . . I meant *it* always to be mystically within and behind them, giving them a significance beyond themselves, forcing itself through them to expression in mysterious words, symbols, actions they do not themselves comprehend. And that is as clearly as I wish an audience to comprehend *it*. *It* is Mystery—the mystery any one man or woman can feel but not understand as the meaning of any event—or accident—in any life on earth. And it is this mystery which I want to realize in the theatre.

I have italicized the word it to underline the shift in reference that takes place. The first two times "it" is "the background pattern of conflicting tides in the soul of man." The third time "it" is just a blur, meaning nothing in particular, exemplifying rather than clearing up the mystery that O'Neill finds important. An event can be mysterious, but how can its mystery be its meaning? And how can we know that its mystery is its meaning if we do "not understand" it? And what would constitute a "realization" of such a phenomenon in the theater?

—Eric Bentley, *In Search of Theatre* (New York: Alfred A. Knopf, 1953): pp. 239–241

Timo Tiusanen on the Effects of Staging on Character Monologue

[Timo Tiusanen has written about the plays of Friedrich Dürrenmatt in addition to his work on Eugene O'Neill. In this selection, Tiusanen discusses O'Neill's use of staging to unify character monologues in *The Iceman Cometh*.]

The Iceman Cometh is essentially a series of modified monologues. They are intertwined and counterpointed, until the final impression is far from static; and their material is richer than in *More Stately Mansions*. There are numerous stage directions in which O'Neill remarks that his characters speak out of inner compulsions and that the listeners are inattentive. Parritt goes on "as if Larry hadn't spoken"; Hickey speaks "staring ahead of him now as if he were talking aloud to himself as much as to them." These are the two characters in whom the inner compulsions are too strong to be subdued by any amount of resistance, not even that furnished by a stage full of antagonistic listeners. Willie Oban and Hugo Kalmar, on the other hand, have the minimum amount of restraint: they emerge from their drunken stupor to shout their thoughts and pass away again. The others are in between; yet all are given an opportunity to reveal their characteristic fluctuation between two different masks.

The dynamics within the speeches are part of the reason why O'Neill was now capable of relying on his dialogue more than ever. The speeches are written in his native tongue—the American vernacular. The changes in the visual stage picture are kept to a minimum: there are three settings, all depicting the same bar with minor variations in the angle. It is worth noticing that even here O'Neill remained truthful to his circle structure: Acts I and IV have the same setting, with a small but significant change in the placement of the chairs, emphasizing Hickey's lonely position. The impression of immobility is further accentuated by keeping stage action to a minimum; most of the time, all the characters are on stage, sitting solidly in their chairs. All these "demobilizing" factors help to keep the attention of the audience focused on O'Neill's music-like handling of his themes.

On the next level, there is an interaction between different characters and groups of characters. Rosamond Gilder in her review of the original production of *The Iceman Cometh* states: "There is little movement; there is only an antiphonal development of themes. . . .

O'Neill's bums . . . spend most of their time in blissful or tormented alcoholic slumber. O'Neill uses this device to bring them in and out of the action without making them leave the stage. As the play progresses, the way the tables are grouped in the backroom and bar and the manner in which actors are grouped around them—slumped over asleep or sitting in a deathly daydream—provides a constant visual comment on the developing theme." Within the realistic framework there is a thematic fluidity which would not be permitted in a tighter play, closer to the formulas of the "well-made play." The coordinating factor is a problem common to all characters—not a plot, in which each should perform his own, highly individual function. The significance of the plot had been diminishing in O'Neill ever since *Ah, Wilderness!*, another indication that *Days Without End* and not the comedy was a digression. *The Iceman Cometh* is, in its orchestral organization of the material, O'Neill's *The Three Sisters*.

The problem of length arises out of necessity. As a matter of fact, it has been actual ever since *Strange Interlude; Mourning Becomes Electra*, a "plotty" and straightforward play, was not as open to criticism as O'Neill's long postwar plays. There is full reason to refer again to the paradox of the O'Neillian length—a paradox seemingly so easily solved with the help of a blue pencil.

—Timo Tiusanen, *O'Neill's Scenic Images* (Princeton: Princeton University Press, 1968): pp. 269–271

CHESTER CLAYTON LONG ON O'NEILL'S USE OF THOUGHT AS A DRAMATIC DEVICE

[Chester Clayton Long is a professor in the Department of Speech at the University of Washington. In this excerpt, Long discusses thought as a poetic medium in *The Iceman Cometh*.]

The action of the play appears to turn around a dead center. At that center seems to be an odd notion of truth. Vivian Hopkins tells us, in her comparison of *The Iceman Cometh* to Gorky's *The Lower Depths*, that:

> O'Neill's analysis of social reform, of course, goes deeper
> than Gorky's. Through Larry he presents the concept
> that a rearrangement of material goods cannot alter
> men's spirit.

But O'Neill does not present an "analysis of social reform". The intent of this play is not didactic, for it implies no workable program to deal with the issues it raises.

Neither does it seem to be a play of character, involving as a synthesizing principle complete alteration in moral character, brought on or controlled by action, and made apparent in itself in thought and feeling. The experience in which all of these characters most frequently participate, just in terms of sheer quantity, is thought. Hickman presents them with the grim challenge of objectively thinking about what they really are. This starts in the first act, and on whatever level of thought they are capable of functioning, they proceed for three acts to *think* about themselves and what they really are, divesting themselves of every one of their illusions in the process. Though Larry and Hickey are the two major characters, all the others indulge in the same activity— driven on by Hickey, and comforted by Larry. ⟨. . .⟩

The possibilities of the poetic medium of thought employed by O'Neill in this play are numerous. The most striking possibility he has used resides in the manifold types of thought he imitates. They range from the thoughts of the low and uneducated to the most elevated and protracted realm of speculation witnessed in the subtly balanced perception of a true thinker, Larry Slade. But these various kinds of thought become centered on one problem in the play: the relative value of truth versus illusion. This is the dead center around which the thought of all the characters revolves.

Most of the characters do not think efficiently about the problem. The two who do are Larry Slade and Theodore Hickman. Hickey's mode of thought is primarily intuitive. He progresses by trial and error. Larry Slade's mode of thought, however, is analytic, depending strictly on evidence, and especially on immediately observed fact. Larry is the scientist; Hickey, the poet-priest. Both men arrive at the truth about *themselves,* however; Hickey by intuitive progression, and Larry by analysis.

Hickey kills his wife under the guise of love. It is his intuition that this has given him a sense of peace and release he has never been able to experience, and assumes that if everyone will face up to himself as he has done (by destroying his pipe dream, which, in his case, was the dream of some day living up to Evelyn's expectations of him), he will find the same peace and freedom. However, he discovers intuitively, through an act of protracted faith in his original intuition, during his long confession to the gang, that his killing his wife was not motivated by love, but by hate. He tells them that he had decided to kill himself so that Evelyn might be spared the continuous pain of his moral defections, but realized instead that if she loved him as much as she seemed to, his suicide would only increase her pain. There was only one course open to him if he were to put an end to her pain, he says, and that was to kill Evelyn. But at the moment he is describing his "mercy" killing, he remembers that he said, "Well, you know what you can do with your pipe dream now, you damned bitch!" His intuitive knowledge is double edged; he has found peace, release, a new lease on life, but it comes from the satisfaction of his hatred, rather than from a fulfillment of his love. And in the end he knows intuitively that other men cannot live with this truth any more than he can; thus, he allows them their pipe dreams, convincing them that he must have been insane.

Larry's case is different. He has spent years in the observation of men, and has inducted the truth from the collective facts of his observations to be that they cannot live without their illusions. He has not known the truth about himself, however. Whereas he had always thought that he loved death, and that he was happily awaiting death, free of all illusions, Hickey, the intuitive thinker, perceives immediately that Larry desperately clings to life, and in reality does not want death. Larry's love of death is also a pipe dream that sustains life, that sets him apart in his own mind, that gives him a false sense of dignity. When Hickey tells him this, Larry is shaken, for the possible power and accuracy of Hickey's intuitive thought has been concretely demonstrated for Larry by Hickey's knowing there is something wrong with Parritt after having seen Parritt for the first time:

> LARRY: For the love of God, mind your own business! (*With forced scorn*) A lot you know about him! He's hardly spoken to you!

HICKEY: No, that's right. But I do know a lot about him just the same. I've had hell inside me. I can spot it in others. (*Frowning*). Maybe that's what gives me the feeling there's something familiar about him, something between us.

At the end of the play Larry realizes that he is truly afraid of death. Proceeding by analysis, he reasons that if his supposed love of death has been the pipe dream that has sustained his life, and that according to the observed facts men cannot live deprived of their illusions, and that he finally has been irrevocably deprived of his illusion, the facts of the case plainly illustrate that he is the only convert to death that Hickey has made; for the others easily take up their pipe dreams again, whereas he cannot, for the power of his thought is too penetrating.

—Chester Clayton Long, *The Role of Nemesis in the Structure of Selected Plays by Eugene O'Neill* (The Hague, the Netherlands: Mouton & Co., 1968): pp. 185–186, 187–189

DORIS FALK ON HICKEY AND LARRY SLADE

[Doris Falk is professor emeritus of English at Rutgers University. She has also written a major volume on Lillian Hellman. In this excerpt, Falk discusses the character of Hickey and his effect on Larry Slade.]

Hickey arrives at the bar on Harry Hope's birthday, an occasion for one of his periodical binges, but instead of the gay and dissolute Hickey they all expect, he is serious and sober. He announces the reason for the change: He has at last found peace by facing the truth about himself. Gradually he shames his listeners into believing that they, too, will find peace if they destroy their illusions and see themselves as they really are. He persuades all except Larry to go forth into the daylight and attempt the social rehabilitation they have always promised themselves. One by one, however, they crawl back to the bar the next day, broken and defeated by inevitable failure. They have faced the truth, but it has robbed them of the last, pitiful trace of hope.

Now not even liquor can make them happy; their old friendships turn to antagonisms. Hickey realizes that his plan has failed, and in trying to explain the failure to himself and to them he reveals that he attained his state of "peace" by killing his wife, Evelyn.

Hickey has convinced himself that he killed his wife because he loved her and wanted to spare her unhappiness over his uncontrollable drunkenness and dissipation—but as he speaks, his real motive comes through. He hated Evelyn because no matter what he did she always forgave him, never punished him, was always faithful. His running gag with the boys at Hope's had been that Evelyn was betraying him "in the hay with the iceman," but this was only his own wishful thinking. She never gave him even this relief from his own guilt. Hickey killed Evelyn because that was the only way he could free himself from her eternal forgiveness and achieve the ultimate in self-punishment. For him, to commit murder was to commit suicide. He has already called the police at the time of his confession.

When the police have arrived, however, and Hickey is concluding his story, his guilt becomes too much for him to face. Ironically, he creates his own pipe dream by persuading himself that he was insane at the moment of the murder. Hickey's illusion is a blessing to his friends, for it restores their own. Now they can go back to their bottles, convinced that they knew Hickey was insane all the time and faced reality only to humor him.

But Larry cannot go back. He must listen to Parritt's confessions—in dramatic antiphony to Hickey's—of his hatred of his mother (caused chiefly by jealousy of her many lovers) which led him to betray her to life imprisonment. Parritt has already resolved upon suicide, but he forces Larry to support his resolution. After listening to Parritt's outpourings, Larry finally cries, "Go, get the hell out of life, God damn you, Before I choke it out of you! . . ." Parritt is relieved and grateful: "Thanks, Larry. I just wanted to be sure. I can see now it's the only possible way I can ever get free from her. . . . It ought to comfort Mother a little, too. . . . She'll be able to say, 'Justice is done! So may all traitors die!' . . ."

—Doris Falk, *Eugene O'Neill and the Tragic Tension: An Interpretive Study of the Plays* (New York: Gordian Press, 1982): pp. 159–161

EDWARD L. SHAUGHNESSY ON EUGENE O'NEILL AND MODERNISM

[Edward L. Shaughnessy is a professor emeritus of English at Butler University, Indianapolis, Indiana. He is the author of *Down the Nights and Days: Eugene O'Neill's Catholic Sensibility* (1996) and numerous essays on O'Neill's family and cultural background. In this excerpt, Shaughnessy examines O'Neill as an "ambivalent modernist."]

For many years frozen into Nietzschean coldness and Strindbergian hardness, in the end the iceman melted. In the wrenching effort to bring forth the play and to immortalize "the four haunted Tyrones," the playwright had wept so profusely that, as his widow recalled, ridges were etched into his face each day as the work continued. Even so, he maintained thematic fidelity: the results were vintage O'Neill.

For his theme had never really changed. Announced as early as 1922 in *The Hairy Ape,* it would be rendered in variations in all of his later plays. One can state that theme very simply: modern man can no longer integrate with his universe; he has lost his old harmony with nature and can find no viable substitute for his lost faith. The individual seeks to know, like Yank (the "ape"), "Where do I fit in?" As he becomes more articulate and sophisticated, like Larry Slade in *The Iceman Cometh,* modern man knows that he no longer does fit in. Thus defeated by his fate, he creates a life lie, the dream that he counts on and upon which he builds the shaky structure of his existence. Such grim philosophy offers but little consolation.

An ambivalent modernist, O'Neill never wrote except with religious intent. He had always been inclined to mysticism but in a way that juxtaposed oddly with his philosophy. For, while he felt the urge to unite with the sublime, he questioned whether there is anything (beyond the horizon) to unite with. (O'Neill would forever feel guilty about this questioning.) But he was also convinced that to believe we belong is our necessary pipe dream, a supportive illusion without which we cannot live. Man's modern tragedy is, then, to seek a higher life but to know that it cannot be attained. This impossible condition, the playwright held, gives modern drama its stature. It represents the closest imitation to the Greeks he could conceive: " . . . one must have a dream, and the Greek dream in tragedy is the noblest ever."

Despair and exaltation, have they not always fused paradoxically in tragedy? In the modern period, however, O'Neill stands as an anomaly—the classicist who said he accepted the melancholy assumptions of recent philosophy, particularly Nietzsche's. Again and again we find his characters sick and poorly integrated with their time and world. Defeated and dodging self-knowledge, they seek escape in pipe dreams. Yet they experience guilt caused by having embraced the illusions in the first place. Such self-deception requires deft rationalization, precisely Larry Slade's point when he says that chasing happiness is a great game. Turning a deaf ear to the ancient maxim, "Know thyself," each feels humiliated in his weakness and becomes, like Edmund Tyrone, "a little in love with death."

If many today look upon guilt as an unhealthy vestige of superstition, O'Neill could not so summarily dismiss it. In his world guilt compels the individual to seek dignity in spite of a sense of his own insignificance. Psychologically his characters cannot accept that insignificance, even if they claim to accept it "rationally." This is a matter of the highest importance because, stripped of his sense of worth, the person becomes merely pathetic. His guilt, then, contributes in large measure to his tragic humanity. Of course, there is nothing new in this view; it had always been that of the tragedian. Moreover, a sense of guilt, as judged in the Christian view, permits the individual to long for redemption. O'Neill's lack of faith in the dogma would not necessarily preclude his recognizing the human meaning of guilt.

—Edward L. Shaughnessy, *Eugene O'Neill in Ireland: The Critical Reception* (New York: Greenwood Press, 1988): pp. 19–20

LAURIN PORTER ON RELIGIOUS ELEMENTS IN *THE ICEMAN COMETH*

[Laurin Porter teaches drama and modern literature at the University of Texas at Arlington and is presently working on a book about Horton Foote. In this selection, Porter discusses the religious overtones of confession and sin in *The Iceman Cometh*.]

⟨A⟩s the play reaches its climax, the real confessions take place and O'Neill's use of ritual becomes more direct. The parallels to Christ's last supper establish the eucharistic ritual as a backdrop to the action of the play, but in Hickey and Parritt's dual confessions we actually see a ritual enacted before our eyes, although it first appears that neither man feels the need of expiating his crime. When, for instance, Parritt confesses to Larry that his motives for betraying his mother weren't patriotic, as he initially insisted, but financial, he seems to feel no remorse for what he has done. The stage directions point out that "he has the terrible grotesque air, in confessing his sordid baseness, of one who gives an excuse which exonerates him from any real guilt." He has been driven relentlessly, first to find Larry and then to make him his confessor, and he clearly wants Slade to discover his crime, but precisely what sin needs absolution is not yet apparent.

It is the same with Hickey, who for much of the play seems anything but the contrite sinner. His first revelation, that his wife is dead, is spoken in quiet tones. When they gasp, stunned, he quickly reassures them that there is no need for this to spoil Harry's party: "There's no reason—You see, I don't feel any grief. . . . I've got to feel glad, for her sake. Because she's at peace. She's rid of me at last." All this is said with "a simple, gentle frankness." Even his confession the next day that Evelyn has been murdered is made "quietly" and "matter-of-factly." His only concern at this point is that the peace he has promised Hope and the others is not taking hold. He "gazes with worried kindliness at Hope" and says, "You're beginning to worry me, Governor. . . . It's time you began to feel happy—." It is only at the end of the second day, when it is clear that Hickey's plan has failed, that his carefully composed facade begins to crumble. His sense of urgency, like Parritt's, reaches a point where a confession clearly must be made.

Both make one last desperate attempt to achieve the peace which has thus far eluded them. In this climactic scene, with Hickey's powerful sustained monologue and Parritt's contrapuntal interjections, both turn to the appropriate parties for forgiveness and understanding: Parritt, to Larry, who, if not his biological father, has come to fulfill that role; Hickey, to Hope and the other boarders, the family he has chosen over his own wife. Parritt has insisted all along that Larry was the only one who could really understand his dilemma—not just because he serves as Don's father, but also because he too has known Rosa's rejection. Hickey instinctively knows he must convince Harry and the others of the necessity of his deed, though he is wrong about his motive. He rationalizes that they, understanding the reason for his peace, will relinquish their own pipe dreams and be equally at rest. Actually, however, he needs them to validate his decision to murder Evelyn, a decision that he has begun to question. Thus their choice of confessors is fitting in terms of the events and relationships of the play.

It is also appropriate in terms of the religious ritual that structures this scene. The Catholic rite of confession is designed to reincorporate the penitent sinner into the mystical body of the church. The priest is efficacious as confessor to the extent that he represents the spiritual community as a whole; this is the source of his power. In the joint confessions of Hickey and Parritt, both priest and community are represented. Larry Slade, who is described at the outset as having a face with "the quality of a pitying but weary old priest's," plays the part of confessor; Harry and his cronies represent the community. ⟨. . .⟩

⟨N⟩either ⟨Parritt nor Hickey⟩ has been willing to admit his true sin. They need absolution, not so much for their crimes as for the motives which inspired them. Both have gradually revealed their secrets, one step at a time, throughout the course of the play, and now the moment of truth-telling is at hand. As Hickey tells his story to Hope and the boarders, and Parritt, in antiphonal fashion, echoes the drummer's confession point by point to Larry, we learn that the real sin, which both have refused to acknowledge, is their hatred.

—Laurin Porter, *The Banished Prince: Time, Memory, and Ritual in the Late Plays of Eugene O'Neill* (Ann Arbor, MI: UMI Research Press, 1988): pp. 68–69

[Stephen A. Black is Professor of English at Simon Fraser
University and the author of *James Thurber: His Masquer-
ades* (1970) and *Whitman's Journeys into Chaos* (1975). He
has published more than 20 articles on O'Neill in journals
such as *The Eugene O'Neill Newsletter, Modern Drama,* and
American Literature. In this selection, Black compares the
philosophies of Hickey and Larry Slade.]

In *The Iceman Cometh* O'Neill composes a huge and vastly complex
dramatic poem. So large is the playwright's vision that it suffuses
The Iceman with several distinct sensibilities including, at least, the
comic, the realistic, and the tragic. O'Neill requires us to think about
the play from any or all of these perspectives. The comic he represents in the fellowship of Harry Hope's regulars; the "realistic" in the
story of Hickey, and in the mode of presenting Hickey, Larry Slade
and Don Parritt; and the tragic, in the fable of Parritt's crime and
punishment. In the last, the topic of this essay, O'Neill shows the
development of Parritt's insight into his crime, a tragic anagnorisis
that leads and permits the youth to seek and accept a fit punishment
and exorcism.

O'Neill shows Parritt forcing Larry to reach his own recognition
by having to watch and participate and understand what Parritt
learns. Anagnorisis brings Larry, at the end, to the thing he has
spent his life resisting, to feel life's infinite sadness and know that
his intellectual searching has blinded him to fundamental facts
that he thought he knew better than most: that existence implies
mortality; and that human understanding, whatever else it may do,
requires us to anticipate our own death.

The bums are dead and refuse to know it. Somewhere along the
way, when a loss gave them an inkling that they had begun to die
the moment they were born, they shut their eyes in dread. They
put their mouths around a bottle, wrapped themselves in the
friendly darkness of the no-hope saloon, and settled in for the slow
death by booze. From dread of death they became walking corpses,
"a lot of stiffs cheating the undertaker" as Hickey says. Because
they so fear death that they cannot acknowledge its reality, the

bums cannot tolerate enough pain to endure ordinary life except in a state of anesthesia.

Hickey has refused to be afraid. If he senses that something in his nature drives him toward death and has made him want for a long time to kill himself, if it is a condition of mortality that something innate drives us all toward death, that doesn't mean nothing can be done. For Hickey there is always something to do, no matter how bored and restless he is made by the thing within. No matter how small the town he can always find something if he keeps moving. If being alone makes him start seeing things in the wallpaper of hotel rooms, he can do something about it. It can't be booze; he can't drink on the job because it gives him his only independent source of self-esteem. Pride in salescraft helps him keep at bay the gradual death by alcohol. By a leap of faith he will defy nature. With a salesman-preacher for a father, it can't be religious faith. It has to be dames. Any old tart will do in a pinch, but for the long run it has to be love, his of Evelyn and Evelyn's of him, to remove death's sting. Prostitutes accept Hickey's nature, Evelyn forgives it. Evelyn's faith in her faithless husband heals the wound nature has made in his nature. A solution as old as the troubadours, it works for Hickey a long time; then it works no longer and the primacy of death asserts itself. As soon as Hickey enters the bar Larry smells the iceman of death on him.

As sensitive to death as Hickey, Larry had once found a faith that combined love of a woman with a utopian ideology, and, like Hickey's leap of faith, it too worked for a while. But the woman's faith had rested less in a lover than in ideology. When love had soured Larry lost the Movement too. Misanthropy confirmed, he turned away from people to booze and pessimistic philosophy as homeopathic cures for dread of death. Like may heal like, he hopes. He thinks to avoid feeling. Above all, Larry is a rationalist.

—Stephen A. Black, "Tragic Anagnorisis in *The Iceman Cometh*," *Perspectives on O'Neill: New Essays,* ed. Shyamal Bagchee (British Columbia: University of Victoria, 1988): pp. 17–18

Plot Summary of
Long Day's Journey Into Night

Long Day's Journey Into Night, widely considered Eugene O'Neill's masterpiece, is a dark dramatization of the hopelessness in the playwright's own family. Evidence of his intent appears in his dedication of the play to his wife, Carlotta, in 1941 (the play was not produced until 1956, three years after O'Neill's death): "Dearest: I give you the original script of this play of old sorrow, written in tears and blood. . . . I mean it as a tribute to your love and tenderness which gave me the faith in love that enabled me to face my dead at last and write this play—write it with deep pity and understanding and forgiveness for all the four haunted Tyrones."

Rather than organizing the drama around a plot or cohesive sequence of events, O'Neill illustrates the single day in which Mary Cavan Tyrone renews a morphine habit and Edmund Tyrone learns that he has tuberculosis. Beyond these two plot points, the four family members—Mary; her husband James; and their two adult sons, Edmund and James Tyrone Jr. (Jamie)—merely try to exist within the confines of their summer home without psychologically and physically destroying themselves and each other. O'Neill's remarkable feat in this play is that he allows the Tyrones to project great love for one another through a thick bog of self-hatred, poisonous resentment, drug addiction, guilt, and utter despair that threatens to suffocate them.

The play opens in August 1912, as Mary and her successful actor husband, James Tyrone, banter lovingly with one another in the living room of their summer home. Their sons soon emerge from the dining room and join in the conversation with the same breezy good humor. But in the interaction among the four—the teasing about Tyrone's real estate deals and his snoring, the comments about the weight Mary has gained, the references to Edmund's health—a strained and unnatural undercurrent gives the audience its first intimations of a deep underlying disturbance that haunts this family.

All three men comment repeatedly on how healthy Mary looks, but although her sickness is alluded to, the precise nature of the illness remains a mystery until well into the second act. At the same time, Edmund's persistent cough and the frequent references to his "summer cold" also suggest a concealed truth. As **Act I** proceeds, the banter quickly turns into scolding and accusations, especially between Tyrone and his oldest son, Jamie. When Mary exits, ostensibly to see to the cook's preparations for that night's dinner, the facade of normalcy and contentment collapses. Out of her presence, the war between Tyrone and Jamie rages openly: the son attacks the father for penny-pinching even in finding a doctor to diagnose Edmund, and Tyrone in turn accuses Jamie of drunkenness and profligacy:

> JAMIE: I earn my board and lodging working on the grounds. It saves you hiring a man.
>
> TYRONE: Bah! You have to be driven to do even that much! (*His anger ebbs into a weary complaint.*) I wouldn't give a damn if you ever displayed the slightest sign of gratitude. The only thanks is to have you sneer at me for a dirty miser, sneer at my profession, sneer at every damned thing in the world—except yourself.
>
> JAMIE (*wryly*): That's not true, Papa. You can't hear me talking to myself, that's all.
>
> TYRONE (*stares at him puzzledly, then quotes mechanically*): "Ingratitude, the vilest weed that grows"!

This scene introduces a pattern of behavior that is continually repeated throughout the play: one family member attacks another; the "victim" defends himself or herself by accusing the attacker; the attacker continues in the same vein; the victim offers a veiled apology or heartfelt explanation; the assailant does not seem to hear it. O'Neill's repetition of this behavior, interrupted by extended moments of self-immolative confession or grand epiphany, achieves a downward-spiraling quality that ends, finally, in a moment of quiet despair at the end of the play.

The subject of Jamie and his father's conversation turns, as it frequently does, to Mary. "She's been so well in the two months since she came home. . . . It's been heaven to me," Tyrone says earnestly. "This home has been a home again. But I needn't tell you, Jamie," he says. Through the dialogue, we gradually learn that Mary has been in rehabilitation for a drug habit and that the "prescription" she needs now is a measure of peace and tranquillity. Tyrone can hardly believe that at the moment when Mary finally seems to be improved, Edmund becomes gravely ill, and he accuses Jamie of having introduced Edmund to dissolute behavior, which has ruined the younger man's health. Jamie in turn blames his father for retaining a "quack" as a family doctor in an effort to save money.

Mary is the only family member who believes that Edmund's illness is a "summer cold"; the others know that it's much more serious than that. Still, they seem less concerned about Edmund's physical health than about the effect his condition will have on Mary's mental health. As Jamie and Tyrone argue, we learn that Mary told her older son that her morphine addiction developed when she became ill after giving birth to Edmund, and her husband sought out a poorly trained, inexpensive doctor. Enraged, Tyrone calls his son an "evil-minded loafer," but the two quickly change their tone and the subject of their conversation as Mary reenters the room.

In several of O'Neill's plays, fog is introduced as a augury of difficult times or situations. Here, Mary refers to the physical fog outside the summer home in a way that portends her slide into addiction and mental illness. "[T]ake advantage of the sunshine before the fog comes back. Because I know it will," she tells Jamie and Tyrone, who are about to go outside and work on the lawn. Just then, Edmund enters the room, having waited for his brother and father to leave. Although ostensibly Mary does not blame Edmund for her suffering, she clearly feels resentment toward him for having become ill, just as she blames Jamie and Tyrone for similar offenses. She is also extremely lonely, claiming to have been forced by her husband to live in a summer home to which she is embarrassed to invite guests. The guilt which she so subtly, expertly, and perhaps unconsciously extracts from them gradually becomes obvious, but in a way it is also the glue that keeps the family together.

The deepest wound Mary has suffered is not morphine addiction or loneliness but the loss of her Catholic faith. She remembers with great longing her years in a convent school, and her fierce dedication to God and the Virgin Mary. "Real life" has bled away her sense of the divine, and she openly acknowledges this void, implicitly blaming it once again on her family, as she tells Edmund in **Act II**:

I've become such a liar. I never lied about anything once upon a time. Now I have to lie, especially to myself. But how can you understand, when I don't myself. I've never understood anything about it, except that one day long ago I found I could no longer call my soul my own. (*She pauses—then lowering her voice to a strange tone of whispered confidence.*) But some day, dear, I will find it again— some day when you're all well, and I see you healthy and happy and successful, and I don't have to feel guilty any more—some day when the Blessed Virgin Mary forgives me and gives me back the faith in Her love and pity I used to have in my convent days, and I can pray to Her again— when She sees no one in the world can believe in me even for a moment any more, then She will believe in me, and with Her help it will be so easy. I will hear myself scream with agony, and at the same time I will laugh because I will be so sure of myself.

The play's concluding monologue, delivered softly by Mary, leaves her loss lingering blackly as the curtain falls. Hers is the most intense (if not also the most selfish and outwardly destructive) pain of the four Tyrones. She has lost her faith, and has succeeded neither in returning to it nor replacing it with something else. Morphine has only speeded the loathsome process of living and facilitated the reverie that makes Mary's past more palatable and tangible to her: "[I]n the spring something happened to me," she says of the event that changed her life for the worse. "Yes, I remember. I fell in love with James Tyrone and was so happy for a time."

While Mary reaches blindly for the comfort of her lost faith, her oldest son, Jamie, slowly becomes strangled by paralyzing despair. He has long since given up on his half-hearted attempt to follow in his father's footsteps as an actor. Tyrone, too, has surrendered hope that his son will ever recover his will, and he is resigned to nagging him continually, almost mechanically, about his drinking, his laziness, and his cynicism.

On this subject, O'Neill was clear: he once refuted the charge that his own brother (also called Jamie) was a cynic by insisting that in order to be cynical, one must have once believed in something. In the character of Jamie, his mother's loss of faith is transmuted to a lack of faith altogether. Jamie hopes only for one thing in life: the recovery of his mother. Her condition causes him intense pain, though the precise source of his guilt is mysterious. When Mary reverts to taking morphine again on this day, all of Jamie's illusions vanish.

The most complex relationship in the play may be that of Jamie and Edmund. Outwardly, they are closest to one another, and Jamie explicitly expresses love and pride for his younger brother. But in a drunken confession—one of several by the play's end—Jamie reveals that his protective love for his brother is mixed with a toxic antagonism, a secret desire to see Edmund fail. Yet O'Neill fashions the confession itself as a perverse act of love:

> You better take it seriously. Want to warn you—against me. Mama and Papa are right. I've been rotten bad influence. And worst of it is, I did it on purpose. . . . You listen! Did it on purpose to make a bum of you. . . . Wanted you to fail. Always jealous of you. Mama's baby, Papa's pet! . . . But don't get [the] wrong idea, Kid. I love you more than I hate you. . . . I run the risk you'll hate me—and you're all I've got left. . . . But you'd better be on your guard. Because I'll do my damnedest to make you fail. . . . Remember I warned you—for your sake. Give me credit. Greater love hath no man than this, that he saveth his brother from himself.

Inseparable from Jamie's jealously of Edmund, however, is his own intense self-hatred. He cannot allow himself to think anything good about himself. As unreachable a character as Jamie is, he exhibits more compassion and humanity, one critic argues, than any of the other characters in the play. On a visit to a local brothel, he takes pity on an overweight prostitute named Violet who is about to be fired and hires her services for the evening, initially just to conduct "a little heart-to-heart talk concerning the infinite sorrow of life." Edmund likes this story, but only partially understands its significance—that Jamie, despite everything he has done, is still human. Like Mary, Edmund, who is O'Neill's depiction of himself, searches without hope for something he has lost, a transcendence he claims that he experienced fleetingly while at sea. He tries to describe the transformative experience to his father, who is impressed with his son's poetic inclinations but saddened by his dark, morbid sensibility.

Tyrone knows that he is now helpless to change the downward spiral of his family, yet he cannot accept the inevitable outcome.

Tyrone's perceived sin is financial miserliness, but he also suffers from emotional and spiritual poverty. The wealth he has accumulated from years of playing the lead role in *The Count of Monte Cristo* has been largely spent on ill-advised investments rather than on his family. He tries to explain to Edmund his persistent fear of the poorhouse. He is the product of a desperately poor family from Kilkenny, Ireland, but financial success has been both a blessing and blight, because a steady income came at the cost of a lifetime spent playing the same role onstage. The opportunity to become a great Shakespearean actor is lost forever to Tyrone.

When Tyrone explains his position, Edmund is moved. "I'm glad you've told me this, Papa. I know you a lot better now," Edmund says. It is impossible to ignore in *Long Day's Journey* that each effort a character makes to receive and bestow forgiveness seems to end in accusation and resentment. Yet they do not stop trying, and Mary declares that such outcomes are almost a product of fate: "None of us can help the things life has done to us. They're done before you realize it, and once they're done they make you do other things until at last everything comes between you and what you'd like to be, and you've lost your true self forever." ✿

List of Characters in
Long Day's Journey Into Night

James Tyrone is the family patriarch, the husband of Mary and the father of Jamie and Edmund. An Irish-born actor, he is the victim of his own financial and critical success. He believes that he has wasted his life playing a worthless but lucrative role, the Count of Monte Cristo, and has missed the chance to be a great Shakespearean actor. Having grown up poor, he is confused and despondent over his sons' squandering of opportunities he has labored to give them, and despairs of his wife's ever recovering from her addiction to morphine.

Mary Cavan Tyrone is the wife of James and mother of Jamie and Edmund. Her addiction to morphine is the great dark secret of the play. She is desperately unhappy and lonely, and she has developed a deep paranoia—accusing her family of watching her suspiciously when they are present and accusing them of abandonment when they flee the tyranny of her bitterness and madness.

James Tyrone Jr. (Jamie) is a dissolute alcoholic, who, at age 33, has given up on an acting career. He is intoxicated most of the time, and seems to have few ambitions or expectations for himself. He does not look beyond the day he is living. He lives at home with his parents, whom he loves and despises. His brother, Edmund, is a source both of pride and guilt for him, since Jamie believes that he has helped to make Edmund who he is.

Edmund Tyrone, the younger son of James and Mary, is the one glimmer of success in the Tyrone household, having literary talent and ambition. Yet he is diagnosed with tuberculosis during the course of the play, diminishing the possibility of any future for the Tyrone family. Edmund is O'Neill's self-portrait; the playwright gives him the first name of an older brother of his own who died in infancy.

Cathleen is the secondary cook and maid in the Tyrone summer home. ✿

Critical Views on
Long Day's Journey Into Night

KENNETH TYNAN ON *LONG DAY'S JOURNEY* AS
AUTOBIOGRAPHY

[Kenneth Tynan was an actor, director, and producer in
British theater and television before becoming the drama
critic for *The Spectator* in 1951. His critical writing has also
appeared in the *Evening Standard,* the *Daily Sketch,* the
Observer, and the *New Yorker.* He was also literary manager
for the National Theatre in London for 10 years. In this
excerpt from a 1958 essay, Tynan suggests that O'Neill's literary greatness emerged from personal pain.]

Eugene O'Neill died five years ago. The eclipse of reputation that
commonly befalls great men as soon as they die has not yet happened to him; and now that *Long Day's Journey into Night* has followed *The Iceman Cometh* into London, I doubt if it ever will.
O'Neill has conquered. We have the measure of him at last, and it is
vast indeed. His work stretches like a mountain range across more
than three decades, rising at the end of these two tenebrous peaks, in
which the nature of his immense, hardpressed talent most clearly
reveals itself. As Johnson said of Milton, he could not carve heads
upon cherrystones; but he could cut a colossus from a rock. Sometimes the huge groups of his imagination stayed stubbornly buried
within the rock; worse, they would sometimes emerge lopsided and
unwieldy, so that people smiled at them—not without reason, for it
is widely felt that there is nothing funnier than a deformed giant.

Many charges, during his lifetime, were leveled at O'Neill by the
cherrystone connoisseurs of criticism. That he could not think; that
he was no poet; that his attempts at comedy were even more pathetic
than his aspirations to tragedy. The odd thing is that all of these
charges are entirely true. The defense admits them: it does not wish
even to cross-examine the witness. Their testimony, which would be
enough to annihilate most other playwrights, is in O'Neill's case
irrelevant. His strength lies elsewhere. It has nothing to do with
intellect, verbal beauty, or the accepted definitions of tragedy and
comedy. It exists independently of them: indeed, they might even
have cramped and depleted it.

What is this strength, this durable virtue? I got the clue to it from the American critic Stark Young, into whose reviews I have lately been dipping. Mr. Young is sometimes a windy writer, but the wind is usually blowing in the right direction. As early as 1926 he saw that O'Neill's theatrical power did not rise from any "strong dramatic expertness," but that "what moved us was *the cost to the dramatist* of what he handled" (my italics). Two years later, reviewing *Dynamo,* he developed this idea. He found in the play an "individual poignancy" to which he responded no matter how tritely or unevenly it was expressed. From this is was a short step to the truth. "Even when we are not at all touched by the feeling itself or the idea presented," he wrote, "we are stabbed to our depths by the importance of this feeling to him, and we are all his, not because of what he says but because saying it meant so much to him."

Thirty years later we are stabbed in the same way, and for the same reason. The writings of *Long Day's Journey* must have cost O'Neill more than Mr. Young could ever have conceived, for its subject is that rarest and most painful of all *dramatis personae,* the dramatist himself.

—Kenneth Tynan, "Massive Masterpiece: *Long Day's Journey Into Night* (1958)," *Eugene O'Neill's Critics: Voices from Abroad,* eds. Horst Frenz and Susan Tuck (Carbondale and Edwardsville, IL: Southern Illinois University Press, 1984): pp. 112–113

John Henry Raleigh on O'Neill's References to *The Count of Monte Cristo*

[John Henry Raleigh is a professor of English at the University of California at Berkeley and the author of *Matthew Arnold and American Culture,* He is also a contributor to *Parisian Review.* In this excerpt, Raleigh examines the influence of *The Count of Monte Cristo* on Eugene O'Neill and his family.]

James O'Neill's entire life, and the life of his family, was dominated by his role in *The Count of Monte Cristo.* He had already been playing it for five years when Eugene O'Neill was born, and Doris

Alexander in her biography of the playwright speculates that the words "Monte Cristo" must have been among the first words that Eugene O'Neill ever heard. We know that he grew up hearing about the play, watching it be rehearsed, and seeing it performed. Later on he was to play a small part in it himself. James O'Neill played the role more than six thousand times; it earned him some $800,000, but it used up an acting talent that at one time anyway was thought to be of the first order. He began playing Dantes in 1883; by 1908 he declared that he was as much a prisoner of the Château d'If as Dantes ever was.

James O'Neill was the fourth of six children in an Irish family that had immigrated to America in 1856. His early life was one of grinding poverty, the father having deserted the family and gone back to Ireland to die. The essential story is told, quite movingly, by James Tyrone in Act IV of *Long Day's Journey into Night*. James O'Neill drifted casually into acting but soon realized it was his destiny. In an age of such great actors as Forrest, Jefferson, and Booth—all of whom O'Neill played with and held his own with—he promised to become one of the most eminent. He knew Shakespeare by heart; he had overcome his brogue; he had good looks, personal charm, a regal bearing, great ambitions, and a splendid voice—"my organ," he called it jokingly. But, like the characters in his son's plays, he was finally balked—by fate, by circumstance, and by himself. The tragedies of James O'Neill's private life have been stressed by his son in *Long Day's Journey into Night*. But, his professional life was, if possible, an even greater tragedy. One of the many reasons that James O'Neill admired Booth was precisely because Booth had managed to surmount private disasters enough to pursue his professional career, always with an admirable reticence about his personal life. But James O'Neill had to add, to his wife's narcotic addiction and to the monumental dissipations and failures of his two sons, the knowledge that his great dramatic gifts had never been fully realized.

On his death bed, agonized by a lingering cancer to which his superb physique long refused to yield, he mumbled to his son: "Eugene—I'm going to a better sort of life—this sort of life—here—all froth—no good—rottenness!" For he had been trapped, as surely as Eugene O'Neill's tragic protagonists are trapped in their respective ways, by the stage version of the Dumas novel. The money he could never resist, and anyway when he tried other roles, serious ones, his audience disappeared. He was finally forced to drain the cup to the last dregs. In 1911, when he was sixty-five years old, he took Dantes on his last tour. The play was by now a tabloid version, condensed below the level of lucidity and merely one of the "acts" in a vaudeville show. It invoked only nostalgia in the audience. Both of his sons, for whom the tour was a prolonged alcoholic binge, were playing parts—no other manager would have hired them—and were given to crude jokes on the stage at their father's expense. He brought his wife, usually in a morphine stupor, to the theater every day because he was afraid to leave her alone in the hotel room. Sometimes she waited in the wings and would become rapt at one of the climactic moments of the play—at the end of Act IV when Mercedes reveals to Dantes, by now the Count, that Albert is their son. At this point Ella O'Neill would begin to move toward the stage like a sleepwalker. She never actually arrived on the stage, but the threat always added to her husband's sense of harassment. In February 1912 *Variety* carried the news that the tour was ended. The Count was finally dead and a splendid acting talent with it.

It is clear, then, that *The Count of Monte Cristo* was not only the millstone around the neck of James O'Neill; it was also all tied up with the life of his family and with its various tragedies: the drunken, irresponsible, vengeful sons misplaying their roles while the stupefied mother haunted the wings like a ghost and the old man, past his prime, tried to hold together a mutilated version of what had been at best only a good melodrama.

The Eugene O'Neill as a playwright was in rebellion against all that *The Count of Monte Cristo* stood for—melodrama, sentiment, easy popularity, stage tricks, cardboard characters, stale rhetoric— is all too obvious. What is not so apparent is how deeply *The Count* was stamped on his creative imagination. His father always obsessed him, and it was impossible to conceive of his father without his father's alter ego, Edmund Dantes. Like his own carving on the balustrade in the house in New London, like the green paint on the statuettes, it was all there, inescapably and almost inexpugnably. If consciously he thought his inspiration derived from Nietzsche, Dostoevski, and Strindberg, which to a considerable degree it did, unconsciously he was often projecting variations on *The Count of Monte Cristo* throughout the whole first part of his creative life.

As a playwright O'Neill had at least two careers. The first career, by which he gained his fame, was played under the shadow of the Château d'If; the second—the one that incorporates *The Iceman Cometh, Long Day's Journey,* and the other late masterpieces—represents, among other things, *his* final escape from the dungeon in which his father lay.

—John Henry Raleigh, "Eugene O'Neill and the Escape from the Chateau d'If (1963)," *O'Neill: A Collection of Critical Essays,* ed. John Gassner (Englewood Cliffs, NJ: Prentice-Hall, Inc., 1964): pp. 7–9

HAROLD CLURMAN ON LOSS AND ISOLATION IN *LONG DAY'S JOURNEY INTO NIGHT*

[Harold Clurman was one of 20th-century America's premier theater critics and directors. He wrote and edited dozens of books on theater and was a critic with a number of journals and newspapers. Clurman's conviction that American theater must become "engaged, passionate, and truthful" led him to assist in forming the Group Theater in 1931. In this selection, Clurman discusses the themes of loss and isolation in *Long Day's Journey Into Night.*]

The four Tyrones are bedeviled by a terrible unnamed loss. The loss inspires guilt in them; they thrash about in a vain effort to identify it, though they hardly realize the nature of their quest. They blame one another for the absence of what is essential to them, and immediately thereafter apologize, knowing that the accusations are misdirected. Each is isolated in his or her sorrowful guilt. Only one of them, Edmund, may emerge from the morass—as Eugene O'Neill did later, through his plays.

The long day's journey is a bitter self-examination into the darkness of the self. The journey for the dramatist constituted a process of self-discovery. But the play's characters, bound together by their dilemma, which makes for a kind of tortured love, are rarely able to touch one another. Each suspects the others of being the cause of his sufferings. An audience sufficiently attentive, and aided by a wholly sound production, should comprehend the source of the Tyrones' tragedy.

They have lost their faith. Loss of faith is the main theme almost throughout O'Neill's work. For him it was more than a personal tragedy, it was *the* American tragedy. As individuals and as a nation, we have lost that spiritual coherence which makes men and societies whole. O'Neill declared that his *magnum opus*—the nine plays, of which he completed only *A Touch of the Poet*—was the dramatization of the question, "What shall it profit a man if he gain the whole world and lose his own soul?"

What innocent and trusting Mary Tyrone has lost is her religious faith, a faith in God which sustained her in the genteel home and the convent in which she was raised. She fell in love with James Tyrone, a star actor of romantically heroic roles, "and was so happy for a time." But the actor in the crude theatre of that day (middle and late nineteenth century), with its long national tours in generally shoddy shows, stopping in every sort of hotel in numerous one-night stands, led a life that offered no haven for so delicate a being as Mary Tyrone. Her husband believed in the theatre, especially in Shakespeare; "I studied Shakespeare," he says, "as you'd study the Bible." Shakespeare was central to his religion, on whose account he rid himself of the brogue of his Irish birth.

But then he found a play which had an enormous success. His many years of immigrant struggle against poverty had made him acutely aware of "the value of a dollar." This turned him to a miserliness to which his sons ascribe all the family's misfortunes. His anxiety to avoid the specter of the poorhouse caused him to abandon his deepest desire to be a great Shakespearean actor and give himself to the exploitation of the box-office hit which he played for more than twenty years to the exclusion of everything else. He betrayed his religion. "What the hell was it I wanted to buy that was worth—" He falters as he asks the question.

The vagrant life of the road led to Mary's intense loneliness (James's boon companions, his fellow actors, were no fit company for such as she) and so unwittingly she became addicted to drugs. On this account, her older son, James, Jr., lost faith in his mother, becoming a cynical drunk and patron of brothels, a blasphemer against his mother's religion and his father's profession, always a little jealous of his younger brother whom he also loves. Edmund is a seeker after truth. He declares himself not so much a poet as a faithful realist. Still, he feels that he will forever be less than whole if he is unable to recapture that sense of belonging to something "greater than my own life, or the life of Man . . . to God, if you want to put it that way. . . ." He experienced such a state at moments in his year at sea. It is this ecstatic relation to existence which Edmund says he lost—"and you are alone, lost in a fog again, and stumble on toward nowhere. . . ."

If the desolateness of this condition in the Tyrone household and the agonized quest for a light beyond the dark are not present in the production, it becomes only the chronicle of an unhappy family—though, even as such, very moving. The triumph is that here a solidly constructed realistic drama is rendered integral with social meaning as well as the soulful poetry of despair and forgiveness. That is what makes *Long Day's Journey into Night* O'Neill's masterpiece.

—Harold Clurman, The Divine Pastime: Theatre Essays (New York: Macmillan Publishing Co., Inc., 1974): pp. 282–284

STEVEN F. BLOOM ON ADDICTION IN O'NEILL'S WORK

[Steven F. Bloom is assistant professor of English and coordinator of the Communication Arts program at Emmanuel College in Boston. He is the author of several articles on O'Neill. In this excerpt, Bloom examines how addictive behavior shapes many of O'Neill's characters.]

One of the most pervasive critical comments about much of Eugene O'Neill's drama is that it is repetitious. Some critics recognize that this repetitiousness is essential to the dramatist's vision, especially in the late plays, yet few seem to appreciate the vital connection between the repetitiousness, the vision, and alcoholism. The life of an alcoholic, after all, is very much defined by repetitious behavioral patterns, and it is in these patterns—in the symptoms and effects of alcoholism—that O'Neill finally discovered a realistic context in which to dramatize his vision of life.

In *Long Day's Journey Into Night,* the realities of alcoholism are vividly depicted in the behavioral patterns of the Tyrone family, collectively and individually, and especially in the dissipation of Jamie Tyrone and the disintegration of Mary Tyrone. Edmund is the romantic idealist, whose visions of transcendence are pointedly couched in terms of romantic notions of blissful intoxication. In the contrast between this romantic myth of intoxication and the realistic symptoms and effects of alcoholism, O'Neill captures the despairing paradox of the human condition, as he sees it.

Three of the four major characters in *Long Day's Journey* become intoxicated by Act IV; the fourth character is under the influence of morphine throughout most of the play. The only other character, Cathleen the servant, is actually drunk most of the brief time she is on stage. Everyone in the play, then, ingests some kind of intoxicant, and the four major characters are, to varying degrees, addicted. This pervasive dependence on chemical substances inevitably affects the behavior of the characters and their interactions in various ways, some subtle and some blatant.

It is important that the symptoms of alcoholism are commonly identified with the symptoms of addiction to chemical substances in general, and that the term "chemical dependency" is used interchangeably with "alcoholism" and "addiction." Furthermore, many of the symptoms of "opioid intoxication" (and morphine is an opioid) are often easily confused with those of alcoholic intoxication. So although Mary Tyrone is addicted to morphine rather than to alcohol, she can still be considered the central addictive figure within the family, and the behavior of this family can be viewed as typical of families of chemically-dependent individuals. ⟨. . .⟩

So effective are the patterns and routines established by the Tyrone family that when one first views or read the play, the true nature of the situation can go unnoticed for a while. Nobody drinks during the first act; there are only a few references to drinking and drunkenness, and these seem rather innocuous; and certainly, all references to morphine are oblique and evasive. Thus *Long Day's Journey* begins as a pleasant, peaceful domestic drama might begin, quite obviously similar, in fact, to O'Neill's own domestic comedy *Ah, Wilderness!* As Henry Hewes remarked in his review of the original New York production of *Long Day's Journey,* "one might assume that this was going to be a comedy about two 'regular fellers' and their happily married mom and dad." It is morning; the family has had breakfast; Tyrone and Mary enter together smiling and teasing each other quite lovingly, with the two sons heard laughing in the dining room. Little is missing, it seems, from the scene of domestic tranquility. As the act progresses, however, we notice hints that all is not well beneath the surface; and that the three men are desperately trying to sustain the calm façade.

The earliest indications of tensions are not directly, explicitly, connected to alcoholism. There is apparently a generational conflict between the father and his two sons, but at first this hardly seems remarkable; there is also obvious concern for Edmund's health and Mary's "nervousness," but the latter is not necessarily drug-related. There is certainly a pattern of defensiveness within the family, as hardly a comment goes by without provoking a defensive reaction from someone. Even Edmund's story about Shaughnessy and the pigs—the kind of story O'Neill often uses in his plays to promote an atmosphere of camaraderie—here leads to an argument with the father pitted against his two sons. For the most part, however, the men make concerted efforts to contain their arguments and to sustain a jocular and amiable atmosphere. That it *is* an effort to do so becomes clear as soon as Mary exits; then, the façade falls and the mood changes drastically.

The anger and defensiveness beneath the surface are now released in a confrontation between father and son that consists of bitter accusations and counteraccusations. The contrast between this scene and the previous one when Mary was present illustrates a pattern within the alcoholic family that the Howards describe ⟨in their article⟩ as typical:

> If the problem drinker appears to be in a pleasant mood and is sober, no one would dare mention anything unpleasant or any drinking behavior, fearing that such a communication would rock the boat and the pleasant mood would be drowned in the resulting anger and defensive response.

—Steven F. Bloom, "Empty Bottles, Empty Dreams: O'Neill's Use of Drinking and Alcoholism in *Long Day's Journey Into Night* (1984)," *Critical Essays on Eugene O'Neill*, ed. James J. Martine (Boston: G. K. Hall and Co., 1984): pp. 159, 160–161

[Judith Barlow is professor of English and Women's Studies at the State University of New York at Albany. In addition to essays on Eugene O'Neill's works, she has also written articles on Lillian Hellman, Tina Howe, and the Provincetown Players, and she is the editor of *Plays by American Women 1900–1930* and *Plays by American Women 1930–1960*. In this excerpt, Barlow discusses the character of Edmund Tyrone and his place in O'Neill's drama.]

Edmund Tyrone is the most controversial character in *Long Day's Journey Into Night*. Critics often divide into two camps: those who believe he is as important as or only slightly secondary to Mary, and those who complain he is the weakest and least interesting figure in the drama. Extraneous biographical considerations sometimes enter the discussion: Edmund is most important because he "is" the young O'Neill or, conversely, Edmund should be central and would be if O'Neill had been as biographically honest about this character as he was about the others. The biographical side of the argument is largely irrelevant; merely incorporated additional personal data would not have solved the problems O'Neill faced in defining Edmund and his place in the family tragedy. The dilemma is dramatic rather than biographical: like *Iceman*'s Larry Slade, Edmund Tyrone's main function is to listen to, learn from, and gain compassion for the other characters. This role is basically a passive one, and all of O'Neill's considerable efforts to gain attention for Edmund could not overcome this fact.

Several issues surrounding Edmund concerned O'Neill as the play progressed: how closely connected he is to the other family members; how guilty he is of transgressions against himself and others; how serious his illness is; and what chance there is for him to escape from the circle of mistakes and betrayals that has entrapped his kin. While the playwright did not drastically change Edmund between the first notes and the published text, the subtle modifications he made are important.

O'Neill's first challenge was to bring Edmund out from under the shadow of the other characters, to make him an individual in his own right. *Journey* reveals that Jamie has deeply influenced his younger brother, but preliminary versions show a far stronger link between the two. Throughout the drafts Mary and Tyrone accuse Edmund of simply mouthing his brother's antagonistic sentiments; they imply that he, with little mind of his own, is scarcely more than a pale copy of Jamie. O'Neill not only canceled many of these accusations, he made other changes that weaken the ties between the Tyrone sons. In his third-act confession, Jamie tells Edmund, "Hell, you're more than my brother. I made you! You're my Frankenstein!" Jamie, making the common mistake of confusing Frankenstein with his monster, suggests that he has created Edmund. Canceled typescript lines go even further, hinting that Edmund is not simply his older brother's creation but virtually a duplicate of him. Jamie asserts, "You're more my son, in a way, than Mama's or Papa's," and a few moments later adds, "You're me. I'm inside you!" The manuscript's and typescript's final scenes have Edmund declaiming one stanza of Swineburne's tearful "A Leave-taking" while Jamie begins and ends the recitation with the second and sixth stanzas. O'Neill subsequently gave all the verses to Jamie, thus separating the two brothers in the audience's mind—a necessary distinction as the drama draws to a close. It is Jamie's poem, an expression of his desolation; Edmund has his own lines in *Journey*'s climactic scene.

O'Neill originally intended the dead baby Eugene to figure more prominently in Mary's ravings. An early note states: "Dead son becomes only child she loved—because living sons cause too much pain—." This idea is carried into the scenario, where Mary laments, "It is too bad [Eugene] could not have lived and we might have had one son we could be proud of." This view of the dead Eugene, which implicitly links Jamie and Edmund as failures, disappears after the scenario. Through revisions O'Neill also weakened connections between Eugene and Edmund. In a deleted typescript passage, Mary complains to her younger son: "I loved you so much because you were you and you were Eugene, too. You took his place. I bore you into the world—in spite of my being so afraid, because I wanted you to take his place." Once again Edmund is denied an identity of his own; he is a substitute for, almost a reincarnation of, his dead sibling. Jamie makes the same point in the manuscript when he charges, "You took Eugene's place" and adds that he is trying to ruin Edmund just as he killed the infant. Eugene does remain in *Journey* as a parallel figure to Edmund but, by deleting these passages, O'Neill blurs the bonds between the two. Mary and Jamie recognize Edmund as a separate person, not just a surrogate for the dead brother he never knew.

Before Edmund could stand alone as an independent character, the alliance between the young man and his mother also had to be diminished. Early versions suggest that Mary's attachment to her younger son is stronger than the published text acknowledges. Throughout the drafts Mary proclaims her preference for Edmund, and this umbilical link seems almost certain to strangle him. The phrases "maternal solicitude" and "motherly solicitude," describing her attitude toward Edmund, occur more frequently in manuscript and typescript stage directions than in the final play. When Mary in the manuscript implies that Edmund's birth caused her misery, she is immediately contrite. "How could it be your fault?" she cries. "How could I blame you! Why, you are my baby still, you mean more to me than anyone, Dear!" Edmund responds with his own declaration: "And you are more to me, Mama." Later in the manuscript a furious Mary informs her husband, "Edmund is mine and I'm going to keep him!" These excised lines demonstrate both her stifling love for Edmund and her feeling that he is less a human being then a cherished possession.

—Judith Barlow, *Final Acts: The Creation of Three Late O'Neill Plays* (Athens, GA: University of Georgia Press, 1985): pp. 97–99

RICHARD B. SEWALL ON O'NEILL'S LITERARY INFLUENCES

[Richard B. Sewall is a professor emeritus of English at Yale University. He is author of *The Vision of Tragedy* and a definitive biography of Emily Dickinson, for which he received the National Book Award. In this excerpt, Sewall reviews O'Neill's literary influences and his concept of tragedy in *Long Day's Journey Into Night*.]

Let me take another route in our attempt to close in on O'Neill and *Long Day's Journey*. This route is by way of Tragedy (with a capital *T*) and the tragic theater. Even here Conrad could have helped him, as witness the somber tone of the preface—the sense of mystery, the pain, the loneliness, the glimpses (but glimpses only) of truth. I don't know how many other novels by Conrad that O'Neill read, but the tragic tone pervades almost all of them, from the death of James Wait on the "Narcissus" (it clearly foreshadows the death of Yank in *Bound East for Cardiff*) to the "mist" that veils the truth about his young hero, Lord Jim, and "the destructive element" that eventually claims him. (The fog in *Long Day's Journey* might well be a descendent of Conrad's metaphor of the mist.) Conrad brought to the novel what O'Neill, historically, brought to the American theater and by much the same route.

From his early years, O'Neill widely read other sources. Greek tragedy, Strindberg, Ibsen, the morose poets whom Edmund and Jamie quote so freely in *Long Day's Journey*—Baudelaire, Dowson, Swinburne, Schopenhauer, Nietzsche, and Dostoevski—added to the tragic set of his mind. He told one of his editors, later, that had it not been for Strindberg's *Dance of Death* and Dostoevski's *Idiot* he might never have begun writing. I would add Conrad.

"The tragic set of his mind." When George Pierce Baker, a professor at Harvard, asked his young friend Eugene O'Neill why he preferred "grim and depressing" subjects for the plays he was writing for the 47 Workshop and suggested that perhaps it was something of a pose, O'Neill, then twenty-six, replied simply, "Life looked that way"—an important clue to what determined the tone and tenor of his entire canon. I like to imagine that young O'Neill turned on his heel.

In my career-long fumbling with the idea of Tragedy, I have come to at least one conclusion: If the set of your mind is not tragic, you'd better not try to write a tragedy. Another young man, twenty-six years of age, tried his hand at it in a play called *The Cenci*—and never tried it again. Later, Mrs. Shelley wrote in explanation: "The bent in his mind went the other way." So did Byron's and Tennyson's, although they both wrote what they called tragedies. Goethe was wisest when he said, "The mere attempt to write tragedy might be my undoing"—this in spite of the fact that there are many tragic elements in *Faust*.

This leads me to a crude but useful distinction between Tragedy and "the tragic." A writer—dramatist or novelist—may have a deep and abiding sense of the tragic and yet never write a full-blown tragedy. But just what is a full-blown tragedy? There is much disagreement. There are very few plays or novels universally accepted as such—a few by the Greeks (notably Sophocles), a few by Shakespeare (even

Hamlet has been questioned), Racine's *Phédre.* A short list indeed, so sharp are the cutting edges of critical theory. Among novelists, Hawthorne, Melville, Dostoevski, Conrad, and Faulkner approach fullness of form. But *tragedy* as a term in criticism is in danger of becoming exclusive and academic. I have found the adjective more useful. It includes most of the values, the dynamics, we're presently concerned with. Miguel de Unanumo's great title *The Tragic Sense of Life*—like O'Neill's reply, "Life looked that way"—gets to the heart of the matter.

"It looks that way" to some, then, and not to others. Temperament is surely a decisive element. Unamuno described the tragic sense of life as a kind of subphilosophy, or prephilosophy, "more or less conscious," not so much flowing from ideas as determining them. O'Neill read books, imbibed attitudes and ideas, took a course under Baker; but it was the temperament he was born with that determined what he took from them. Here is Conrad on temperament (again from the preface): "Fiction—if it at all aspires to be art—appeals to temperament. And in truth it must be, like painting, like music, like all art, the appeal of one temperament to all the other innumerable temperaments whose subtle and resistless power endows passing events with their true meaning." O'Neill spoke in much the same way twenty years after his *Cardiff* was first produced (1916), only here he used the terms *spirit* and *life-attitude:* "In it [*Cardiff*] can be seen, or felt, the germ of the spirit, life-attitude, etc., of all my more important future work."

—Richard B. Sewall, "Eugene O'Neill and the Sense of the Tragic (1991)," *Eugene O'Neill's Century: Centennial Views on America's Foremost Tragic Dramatist,* ed. Richard F. Moorton Jr. (New York: Greenwood Press, 1991): pp. 5–6

MICHAEL MANHEIM ON JAMIE TYRONE

[Michael Manheim is a professor emeritus of English at the University of Toledo. He is the author of *Eugene O'Neill's New Language of Kinship* (1982) and *The Weak King: Dilemma in the Shakespearean History Play* (1973); he has also written numerous related articles for journals such as *Shakespeare Studies* and *Renaissance Drama*. Here, Manheim examines Jamie Tyrone as the most humane character in O'Neill's play.]

Jamie Tyrone is the one truly humane figure in this play—and while this idea might seem incomprehensible to some, it contributes much to the kind of stature the play possesses. This stature has to do with the deepest kind of emotional suffering accompanied by the recognition and understanding of that suffering by the sufferer. When Jamie says early in the play that he knows how his father feels about Mary's condition, he speaks out of an empathy which is his unique gift. Along with the large capacity of his own suffering, he can feel the suffering of others—even Mary's, whose drug dependency he is the only one of the three men can see is parallel to his own alcohol dependency. And her reversion, after a brief period of false hope, has hurt him the most: "It meant so much. I'd begun to hope, if she'd beaten the game, I could, too."

The segment of the episode that tells us most about who Jamie is (how O'Neill sees him) is his rendition of this visit to the bordello, where he chose as his sexual companion "Fat Violet," the whore who is about to be let go because none of the customers want her. Though speaking sarcastically (which is his wont), Jamie's description of his time with her as a "Christian act" is in fact just that. He felt *sorry* for Vi, he says—sorry for *her* when his purpose in going to the brothel was to make him forget his sorrow for himself. The fact of having had sex with her especially fits this definition. He had, he says, "no dishonorable intentions" when he escorted her upstairs. He just wanted, he says, to recite some of the modern poets to her (for example, Dowson's "I have been faithful to thee, Cynara, in my fashion")—which characteristically seems intended both to mock her and to comfort her—but she grew angry and cried. "So I had to say I loved her because she was fat," he says, "and she wanted to believe that, and I stayed with her to prove it, and that cheered her up . . ." If the "Christianity" of this act may elude some, it may nevertheless be seen as the one act of completely selfless giving in the play.

Yet with all this, the swings to the negative in Jamie's attitudes become ever more savage—the liquor talking, he says, but we know by this time it is always the essential character talking. He persistently returns to his attacks on Edmund—"Mama's baby, Papa's pet, the family white hope"—even to the most savage of all—"it was your being born that started Momma on dope." But he always swings back to the equally heartfelt praise of his brother and pleas for his understanding: "You're the only pal I've ever had. I love your guts. I'd do anything for you!"

These swings culminate, of course, in his concluding confession, in which he cuts his lifeline with his only friend by warning Edmund of his potentially destructive nature. He will, he says, be waiting to greet Edmund with a genuinely glad hand upon his return from the sanatorium, but he will also be waiting to stab him in the back. This is by no means a confession of hypocrisy but rather an understanding, not shared by the other men about themselves or him, that there are always two parts of an individual speaking, a dead part and a live part: "The dead part of me hopes you won't get well." But while the dead part is to be feared, the live part is equally potent as is revealed in his repeated outbursts of unconditional affection for his brother culminating in his final appeal: "Remember I warned you—for our sake. Give me credit. Greater love hath no man than this, that he saveth his brother from himself." Having Jamie recite this last variant of scripture sarcastically, as some productions do, misses the point. His devotion to Edmund is real, as even James, Sr. observes a few lines later, and it is in his case a devotion the live part of him has for all the people of the play—including Mary. But it is ever juxtaposed with the savagery of the dead part. It is thus that Jamie is O'Neill's spokesman in the play, his exaggeratedly contradictory states focusing tragedy's inescapable light on the human condition.

—Michael Manheim, "The Stature of *Long Day's Journey Into Night*," *The Cambridge Companion to Eugene O'Neill*, ed. Michael Manheim (Cambridge, U.K.: Cambridge University Press, 1998): pp. 214–215

JEAN CHOTHIA ON O'NEILL'S PERSONAL EXPERIENCES AS
DRAMA IN *LONG DAY'S JOURNEY INTO NIGHT*

[Jean Chothia is a lecturer in the Faculty of English at Cambridge University and is Fellow of Selwyn College. She is
author of *Forging a Language: A Study of the Plays of Eugene
O'Neill* (1979), *Andre Antione* (1991), and *English Drama
1890–1940* (1996). In this selection, Chothia discusses the
autobiographical aspects of *Long Day's Journey Into Night*.]

When O'Neill wrote in the dedication to *Long Day's Journey Into
Night*, that he had faced his dead at last in this play written with
"deep pity and understanding and forgiveness for *all* the four
haunted Tyrones," making clear the close identification of the characters and events of the play with his own family history, he indi-
cated that he had, indeed, finally, in this very late work, "mustered
the nerve." Given this, it is remarkable that, apart from the dedication itself, there is no sense for the reader or the theatre audience, of
voyeurism, of encountering experience too personal or too raw. It
takes unusual personal courage to kick away the ladders and sup-
ports of fictional disguise and lie down, as W. B. Yeats has it, "where
all the ladders start, / In the foul rag and bone shop of the heart." But
it also takes art of a very high order to so recreate the private and the
personal in the public medium which drama is that it seems both
truthful and compelling to its audience, that it achieves intensity
without embarrassment and leaves no impression of special
pleading. Ben Johnson's short poem, "On My First Son," cannot fail
to touch the reader as an utterance of intense and uncontrived grief,
and yet it is a most complexly wrought piece of writing. For all the
extremity of some aspects of the experience, it is the literary and
dramatic skill when casting it in convincing dramatic form that
allows O'Neill's late plays to speak to the responding imaginations of
their audiences. And it is with this that I am concerned here.

The direct engagement with autobiography came late but, from
the outset, O'Neill's plays were concerned with secrets and conceal-
ment: with dysfunctional families, isolated from the rest of the community, or with single men, emotionally damaged, in retreat from
the dysfunctional family or haunted by the memory of relationship
that has foundered, and so doomed to wander and to find tempo-
rary consolation in alcohol. Some plays—*Desire Under the Elms, All*

God's Chillun Got Wings, Mourning Becomes Electra, Long Day's Journey Into Night—center the one; some—"The SS Glencairn Plays," *The Hairy Ape, The Iceman Cometh*—center the other, but virtually all include at least elements of both. The fictive locales O'Neill creates within the theatrical space derive directly from these basic situations. Two kinds of setting, seemingly opposed but, in fact, only opposite sides of the same coin, recur: they are notably private spaces—the center, usually the living room, of a family home— or they are notably public spaces—the hold of a tramp steamer, a bar, a flop-house, where disparate people are gathered randomly. The one type culminates in the set of *Long Day's Journey Into Night* which, it is now known, recreates the living room of the O'Neill's New London summer home. The other culminates in the set of *The Iceman Cometh*—an amalgam of the flop-house in which as a young man O'Neill sought escape from self and past.

The more one encounters O'Neill's work the more astonishing the range of setting, plot, character seems, and the more remarkable the extent of the dramatic and theatrical experimentation. But, just as O'Neill engaged in a lifelong and often agonized experimentation with language which came to remarkable fruition in the variousness and seemingly complete naturalness of the densely packed, artful and expressive dialogue of the late plays, so, simultaneously, his own emotional experience, sometimes thinly, sometimes deeply disguised, and disguised perhaps even from himself, is the recurrent subject of plays throughout his writing life. With hindsight, the whole career can be read as a clearing of the ground, a sifting of events, a honing of language and structure in preparation for the extraordinary dramatic control and self-exploration of the final three plays. As certain tropes and motifs are worked and reworked in the changing circumstances of successive plays, the more fully evident it is that, as Michael Manheim has put it, "O'Neill had been writing versions of *Long Day's Journey Into Night* throughout his entire career."

—Jean Chothia, "Trying to Write the Family Play: Autobiography and the Dramatic Imagination," *The Cambridge Companion to Eugene O'Neill*, ed. Michael Manheim (Cambridge, U.K.: Cambridge University Press, 1998): pp. 192–194

Works by
Eugene O'Neill

Thirst and Other One Act Plays. 1914.

Before Breakfast. 1916.

The Moon of the Caribbees and Six Other Plays of the Sea. 1919.

Beyond the Horizon. 1920.

The Emperor Jones. 1921.

Gold. 1921.

The Emperor Jones; Diff'rent; The Straw. 1921.

Plays. 1922.

The Hairy Ape; Anna Christie; The First Man. 1922.

Beyond the Horizon and Gold. 1924.

Complete Works. 1924. 2 vols.

All God's Chillun Got Wings; Desire Under the Elms; Welded. 1925.

Plays. 1925. 10 vols.

Desire Under the Elms. 1925.

The Great God Brown; The Fountain; The Moon of the Caribbees, and Other Plays. 1926.

Marco Millions. 1927.

Lazarus Laughed. 1927.

Strange Interlude. 1928.

The Emperor Jones; Straw. 1928.

Lazurus Laughed and Dynamo. 1929.

The Hairy Ape. 1929.

Dynamo. 1929.

Anna Christie. 1930.

Mourning Becomes Electra. 1931.

Representative Plays. 1932.

Nine Plays. 1932.

Ah, Wilderness! 1933.

Ah, Wilderness! and Days without End. 1934.

Days without End. 1934.

Plays (Wilderness Edition). 1934–35. 12 vols.

Ah, Wilderness! and Two Other Plays. c. 1936.

The Emperor Jones; Anna Christie; The Hairy Ape. 1937.

Plays. 1941. 3 vols.

Selected Plays. 1944.

The Iceman Cometh. 1946.

Lost Plays. 1950.

A Moon for the Misbegotten. 1952.

Long Day's Journey Into Night. 1956.

A Touch of the Poet. 1957.

Hughie. 1959.

Inscriptions: Eugene O'Neill to Carlotta Monterey O'Neill. 1960.

Ten "Lost" Plays. 1964.

More Stately Mansions. 1964.

Selected Plays. 1967.

"Children of the Sea" and Three Other Unpublished Plays. Ed. Jennifer McCabe Atkinson. 1972.

The Last Will and Testament of an Extremely Distinquished Dog. 1972.

Four Plays. 1978.

Poems 1912–1942. Ed. Donald Gallup. 1979.

Selected Plays. 1979.

Eugene O'Neill at Work: Newly Released Ideas for Plays. Ed. Virginia Floyd. 1981.

The Calms of Capricorn. Ed. Donald Gallup. 1981.

Work Diary 1924–43. Ed. Donald Gallup. 1981. 2 vols.

"The Theatre We Worked For": Letters to Kenneth Macgowan. Eds. Jackson R. Bryer and Ruth M. Alvarez. 1982.

Chris Christopherson. 1982.

Works about
Eugene O'Neill

Ahuja, Chapman. *Tragedy, Modern Temper, and O'Neill*. Atlantic Highlands, NJ: Humanities Press, 1983.

Alexander, Doris. *Eugene O'Neill's Creative Struggle: The Decisive Decade, 1924–1933*. University Park: Penn State University Press, 1992.

Bagchee, Shyamal, ed. *Perspectives on O'Neill: New Essays*. British Columbia, Canada: University of Victoria, 1988.

Barlow, Judith. *Final Acts: The Creation of Three Late O'Neill Plays*. Athens, GA: University of Georgia Press, 1985.

Bentley, Eric. *In Search of Theatre*. New York: Alfred A. Knopf, 1953.

Berlin, Normand. *Eugene O'Neill*. New York: St. Martin's Press, 1988.

Bloom, Harold, ed. *Eugene O'Neill*. New York: Chelsea House Publishers, 1987.

———. *Eugene O'Neill's Long Day's Journey Into Night*. New York: Chelsea House Publishers, 1988.

———. *Eugene O'Neill's The Iceman Cometh*. New York: Chelsea House Publishers, 1987.

Bogard, Travis. *Contour in Time: The Plays of Eugene O'Neill*. New York: Oxford University Press, 1988.

Boulton, Agnes. *Part of a Long Story*. Garden City, NY: Doubleday, 1958.

Bowen, Croswell, and Shane O'Neill. *The Curse of the Misbegotten: A Tale of the House of O'Neill*. New York: McGraw-Hill, 1959.

Carpenter, Frederic I. *Eugene O'Neill*. Boston: Twayne Publishers, 1979.

Chabrowe, Leonard. *Ritual and Pathos: The Theatre of Eugene O'Neill*. Lewisburg, PA: Bucknell University Press, 1976.

Chothia, Jean. *Forging a Language: A Study of the Plays of Eugene O'Neill*. New York: Cambridge University Press, 1979.

Clark, Barrett H. *Eugene O'Neill: The Man and His Plays*. New York: Dover Publications, 1947.

Clark, B. H., and Ralph Sanborn. *A Bibliography of the Works of Eugene O'Neill Together with the Collected Poems of Eugene O'Neill*. London: Benjamin Blom, 1965.

Clurman, Harold. *The Divine Pastime: Theatre Essays.* New York: Macmillan Publishing Co., 1974.

Cunningham, Frank. *Sidney Lumet: Film and Literary Vision.* Lexington, KY: University of Kentucky Press, 1991.

Dubost, Thierry. *Struggle, Defeat, or Rebirth: Eugene O'Neill's Vision of Humanity.* Jefferson, NC: McFarland and Company, 1996.

Eisen, Kurt. *The Inner Strength of Opposites: O'Neill's Novelistic Drama and the Melodramatic Imagination.* Athens, GA: University of Georgia Press, 1994.

Engel, Edwin. *The Haunted Heroes of Eugene O'Neill.* Cambridge, MA: Harvard University Press, 1953.

Estrin, Mark W., ed. *Conversations with Eugene O'Neill.* Oxford, MS: University of Mississippi Press, 1990.

Falk, Doris V. *Eugene O'Neill and the Tragic Tension: An Interpretive Study of the Plays.* New York: Gordian Press, 1982.

Floyd, Virginia, ed. *Eugene O'Neill: A World View.* New York: Frederick Ungar, 1979.

———. *The Plays of Eugene O'Neill: A New Assessment.* New York: Frederick Ungar, 1985.

Frazer, Winifred D. *Love as Death in* The Ice Man Cometh: *A Modern Treatment of an Ancient Theme.* Gainsville, FL: University of Florida Press, 1967.

Frenz, Horst. *Eugene O'Neill.* New York: Frederick Ungar, 1971.

Frenz, Horst, and Susan Tuck, eds. *Eugene O'Neill's Critics: Voices from Abroad.* Carbondale, IL: Southern Illinois University Press, 1984.

Gassner, John. *Eugene O'Neill.* Minneapolis: University of Minnesota Press, 1965.

Gassner, John, ed. *O'Neill: A Collection of Critical Essays.* Englewood Cliffs, NJ: Prentice-Hall, 1964.

Geddes, Virgil. *The Melodramadness of Eugene O'Neill.* Brookfield, CT: Brookfield Players, 1934.

Gelb, Arthur, and Barbara Gelb. *O'Neill.* New York: Harper and Row, 1962.

Glaspell, Susan. *The Road to the Temple.* London: Benn, 1926.

Griffen, Ernest G., ed. *Eugene O'Neill: A Collection of Criticism.* New York: McGraw-Hill, 1976.

Hall, Ann C. *"A Kind of Alaska": Women in the Plays of O'Neill, Pinter, and Shepard.* Carbondale, IL: Southern Illinois University Press, 1993.

Hinden, Michael. *"Long Day's Journey Into Night": Native Eloquence.* Boston: G. K. Hall, 1990.

Houchin, John H., ed. *The Critical Response to Eugene O'Neill.* Westport, CT: Greenwood Press, 1993.

Josephson, Lennart. *A Role: O'Neill's Cornelius Melody.* Stockholm: Almquist and Wiksell International, 1977.

Kobernik, Mark. *Semiotics of Drama and the Style of Eugene O'Neill.* Amsterdam: Benjamins, 1989.

Leech, Clifford. *Eugene O'Neill.* London: Oliver and Boyd, 1963.

Liu, Haiping, and Lowell Swortzell, eds. *Eugene O'Neill in China: An International Centenary Celebration.* Westport, CT: Greenwood Press, 1992.

Long, Chester Clayton. *The Role of Nemesis in the Structure of Selected Plays by Eugene O'Neill.* The Hague: Mouton and Co., 1968.

McDonough, Edwin J. *Quintero Directs O'Neill.* Chicago: A Capella Books, 1991.

Manheim, Michael. *The Cambridge Companion to Eugene O'Neill.* Cambridge, U.K.: Cambridge University Press, 1998.

————. *Eugene O'Neill's New Language of Kinship.* Syracuse, NY: Syracuse University Press, 1982.

Martine, James J., ed. *Critical Essays on Eugene O'Neill.* Boston: G. K. Hall, 1984.

Maufort, Marc, ed. *Eugene O'Neill and the Emergence of American Drama.* Amsterdam: Rodopi, 1989.

————. *Songs of American Experience: The Vision of O'Neill and Melville.* New York: Peter Lang, 1990.

Miller, Jordan Y. *Eugene O'Neill and the American Critic.* Hamden, CT: Archon Books, 1973.

Moorton Jr., Richard F., ed. *Eugene O'Neill's Century: Centennial Views on America's Foremost Tragic Dramatist.* Westport, CT: Greenwood Press, 1991.

Orlandello, John. *O'Neill on Film.* Rutherford, NJ: Fairleigh Dickinson University Press, 1982.

Pfister, Joel. *Staging Depth: Eugene O'Neill and the Politics of Psychological Discourse.* Chapel Hill, NC: University of North Carolina Press, 1995.

Porter, Laurin R. *The Banished Prince: Time, Memory, and Ritual in the Late Plays of Eugene O'Neill.* Ann Arbor, MI: UMI Research Press, 1988.

Prasad, Hari. *The Dramatic Art of Eugene O'Neill.* New York: Advent Press, 1987.

Raleigh, John Henry. *The Plays of Eugene O'Neill.* Carbondale, IL: Southern Illinois University Press, 1965.

Ranald, Margaret Loftus. *The Eugene O'Neill Companion.* Westport, CT: Greenwood Press, 1984.

Robinson, James A. *Eugene O'Neill and Oriental Thought: A Divided Vision.* Carbondale, IL: Southern Illinois University Press, 1982.

Scheibler, Rolf. *The Late Plays of Eugene O'Neill.* Bern, Switzerland: Francke Verlag, 1970.

Shaeffer, Louis. *O'Neill: Son and Artist.* Boston: Little, Brown, 1973.

Shaughnessy, Edward L. *Eugene O'Neill in Ireland: The Critical Reception.* New York: Greenwood Press, 1988.

Sinha, C. P. *Eugene O'Neill's Tragic Vision.* Atlantic Highlands, NJ: Humanities, 1981.

Skinner, Richard Dana. *Eugene O'Neill: A Poet's Quest.* New York: Longman's Green, 1935.

Stroupe, John, ed. *Critical Approaches to O'Neill.* New York: AMS Press, 1988.

Tiusanen, Timo. *O'Neill's Scenic Images.* Princeton, NJ: Princeton University Press, 1968.

Tornqvist, Egil. *A Drama of Souls: O'Neill's Studies in Supernaturalistic Technique.* New Haven, CT: Yale Univeristy Press, 1969.

Vena, Gary. *O'Neill's* The Iceman Cometh: *Reconstructing the Premiere.* Ann Arbor, MI: UMI Research Press, 1988.

Wainscott, Ronald H. *Staging O'Neill: The Experimental Years, 1920–1934.* New Haven, CT: Yale University Press, 1988.

Winther, Sophus Keith. *Eugene O'Neill: A Critical Study.* New York: Russell and Russell, 1961.

Index of
Themes and Ideas